MW01013551

MASTER BASIC FRACTION SKILLS

WORKBOOK

DR. PI SQUARED

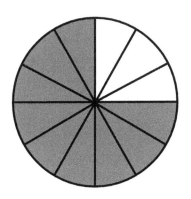
$$\frac{9}{12} = \frac{3}{4}$$
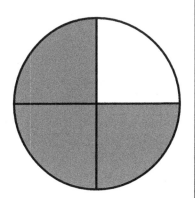

Master Basic Fraction Skills Workbook
Dr. Pi Squared

© 2011
Dr. Pi Squared Math Workbooks

Nonfiction/children's/mathematics/arithmetic
Nonfiction/education/mathematics/arithmetic

ISBN-10: 1463567413
ISBN-13: 978-1463567415

Contents

1 Determining Fractions Visually

Basic Concepts: An **integer** is a whole number. Each number in the following sequence is an integer: 0,1,2,3,4,5,6,7,8,9,10,11,12,13, ... A **fraction** is a number that comes between two integers. For example, $\frac{1}{2}, \frac{2}{3}, \frac{4}{7}, \frac{3}{2}, \frac{7}{4}$, and $\frac{9}{2}$ are all fractions. The fractions $\frac{1}{2}, \frac{2}{3}$, and $\frac{4}{7}$ come between the integers 0 and 1. The fractions $\frac{3}{2}$ and $\frac{7}{4}$ come between the integers 1 and 2. The fraction $\frac{9}{2}$ comes between the integers 4 and 5.

You can visually represent an integer as a number of whole pies. For example, the integer 4 is represented below as 4 whole pies.

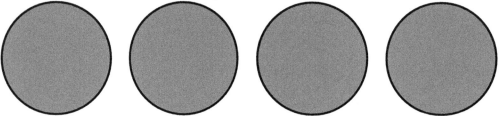

A fraction can't be represented as a whole number of pies, but must be represented with slices of pies. For example, the fraction $\frac{3}{5}$ is illustrated below by dividing a pie into 5 slices and shading 3 of them.

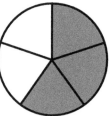

A **mixed number** includes an integer together with a fraction. For example, the mixed number $2\frac{1}{2}$ means two and a half. The mixed number $2\frac{1}{2}$ is illustrated below as two and one-half pies.

Sometimes, a fraction may be written more than one way. For example, one-half of each pie below is shaded gray. This shows that $\frac{2}{4}$ is equal to $\frac{1}{2}$. We will explore this concept further in Chapter 5. For now, this explains why there may be more than one answer in the back of the book for the Chapter 1 exercises.

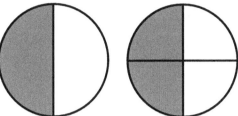

Directions: Write a fraction in each blank that represents the fraction of the pie that is shaded the specified color (gray or white). Study the examples below before you begin. Check your answers in the back of the book.

Example 1. In each blank, write the fraction of the pie that is shaded gray and white.

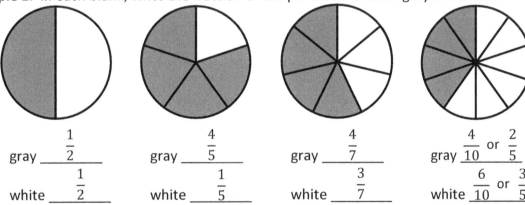

gray ___ $\frac{1}{2}$ ___   gray ___ $\frac{4}{5}$ ___   gray ___ $\frac{4}{7}$ ___   gray $\frac{4}{10}$ or $\frac{2}{5}$

white ___ $\frac{1}{2}$ ___   white ___ $\frac{1}{5}$ ___   white ___ $\frac{3}{7}$ ___   white $\frac{6}{10}$ or $\frac{3}{5}$

Example 2. Write a mixed fraction corresponding to the fraction of the pies that are shaded gray.

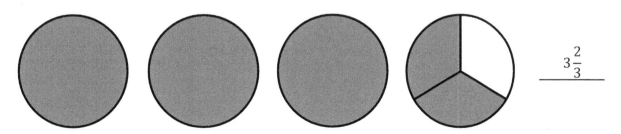

$3\frac{2}{3}$
___

In each blank, write the fraction of the pie that is shaded gray and white.

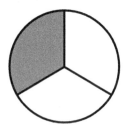 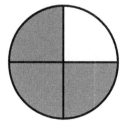 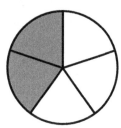 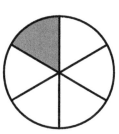

gray _____   gray _____   gray _____   gray _____

white _____   white _____   white _____   white _____

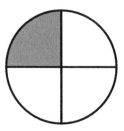 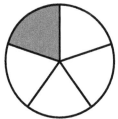 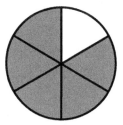 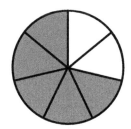

gray _____   gray _____   gray _____   gray _____

white _____   white _____   white _____   white _____

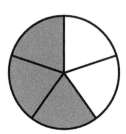 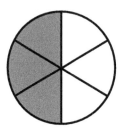 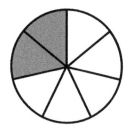 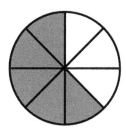

gray _____   gray _____   gray _____   gray _____

white _____   white _____   white _____   white _____

In each blank, write the fraction of the pie that is shaded gray and white.

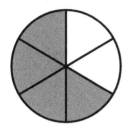 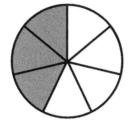 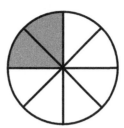 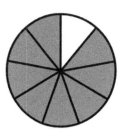

gray _____   gray _____   gray _____   gray _____

white _____   white _____   white _____   white _____

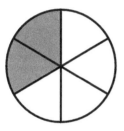 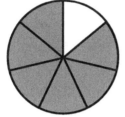 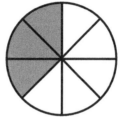 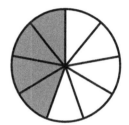

gray _____   gray _____   gray _____   gray _____

white _____   white _____   white _____   white _____

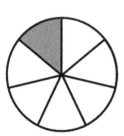 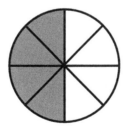 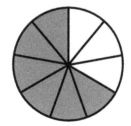 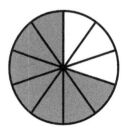

gray _____   gray _____   gray _____   gray _____

white _____   white _____   white _____   white _____

In each blank, write the fraction of the pie that is shaded gray and white.

gray _____

white _____

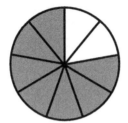

gray _____

white _____

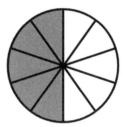

gray _____

white _____

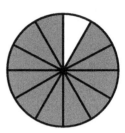

gray _____

white _____

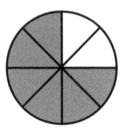

gray _____

white _____

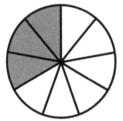

gray _____

white _____

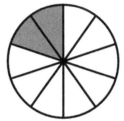

gray _____

white _____

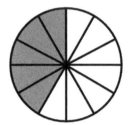

gray _____

white _____

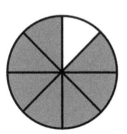

gray _____

white _____

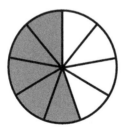

gray _____

white _____

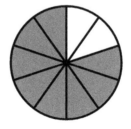

gray _____

white _____

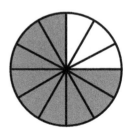

gray _____

white _____

In each blank, write the fraction of the pie that is shaded gray and white.

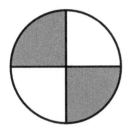 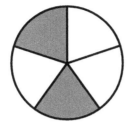 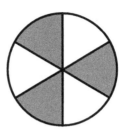 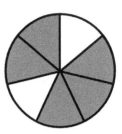

gray _____   gray _____   gray _____   gray _____

white _____   white _____   white _____   white _____

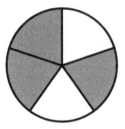 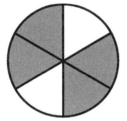 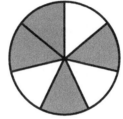 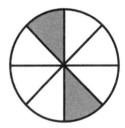

gray _____   gray _____   gray _____   gray _____

white _____   white _____   white _____   white _____

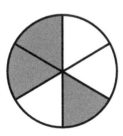 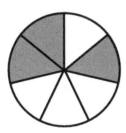 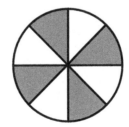 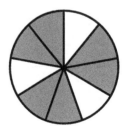

gray _____   gray _____   gray _____   gray _____

white _____   white _____   white _____   white _____

In each blank, write the fraction of the pie that is shaded gray and white.

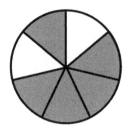

gray _____

white _____

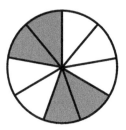

gray _____

white _____

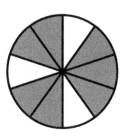

gray _____

white _____

gray _____

white _____

gray _____

white _____

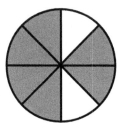

gray _____

white _____

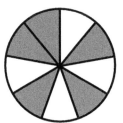

gray _____

white _____

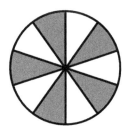

gray _____

white _____

gray _____

white _____

gray _____

white _____

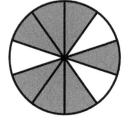

gray _____

white _____

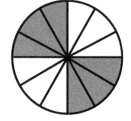

gray _____

white _____

In each blank, write the fraction of the pie that is shaded gray and white.

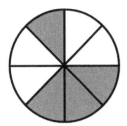

gray _____

white _____

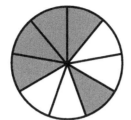

gray _____

white _____

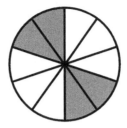

gray _____

white _____

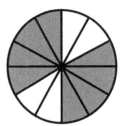

gray _____

white _____

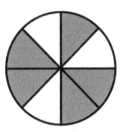

gray _____

white _____

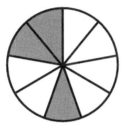

gray _____

white _____

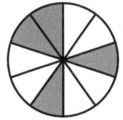

gray _____

white _____

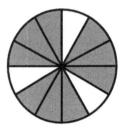

gray _____

white _____

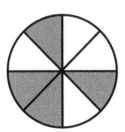

gray _____

white _____

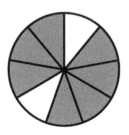

gray _____

white _____

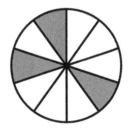

gray _____

white _____

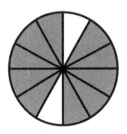

gray _____

white _____

Write a mixed fraction corresponding to the fraction of the pies that are shaded gray.

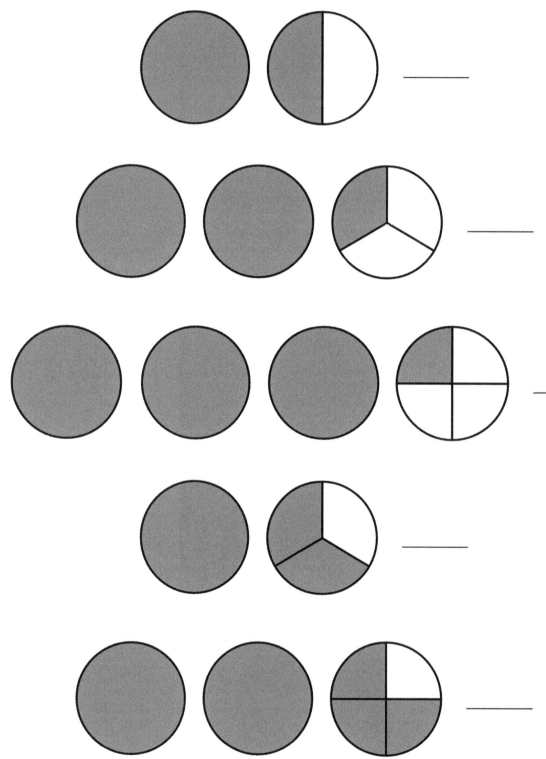

Write a mixed fraction corresponding to the fraction of the pies that are shaded gray.

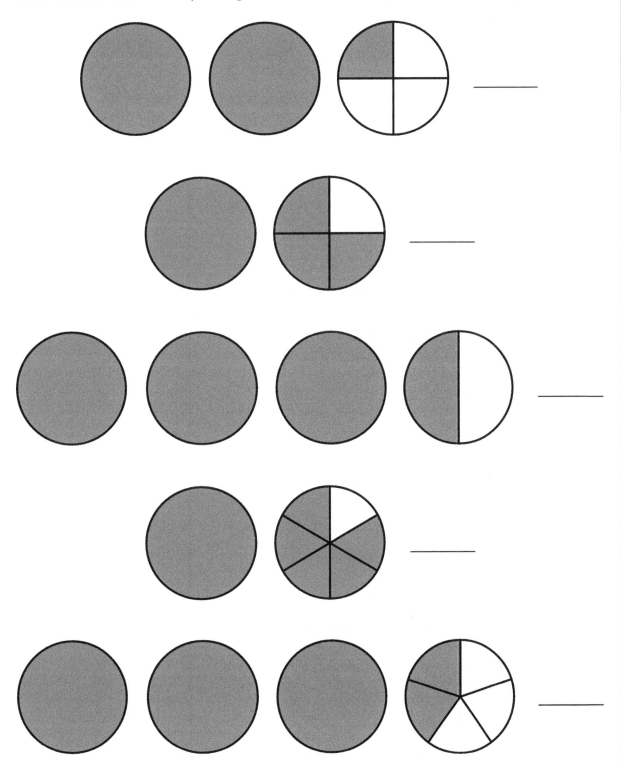

2 Representing Fractions Visually

Basic Concepts: Suppose that a pie is divided up into 9 slices, like the pie shown on the left below, and you are asked to color $\frac{1}{3}$ of them. This means to color 1 out of every 3. Therefore, coloring $\frac{1}{3}$ of the slices means to color 3 of the 9 slices, as illustrated on the pie on the right.

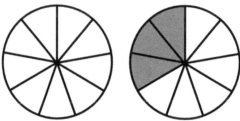

Directions: There are two types of exercises in this chapter. The first type includes blank pies and asks you to color a specified fraction of the pie. The second type asks you to draw a mixed number of pies, like $2\frac{1}{4}$ pies. Both types of questions are just like the exercises from Chapter 1, except that this time you do the drawing. Study the examples below before you begin. Check your answers in the back of the book.

Example 1. Color the correct number of pie slices to match the given fraction.

$$\frac{1}{2} \qquad\qquad \frac{2}{3} \qquad\qquad \frac{1}{3} \qquad\qquad \frac{2}{7}$$

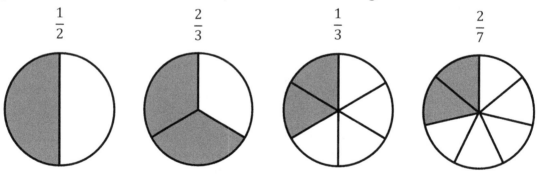

Example 2. Draw $2\frac{1}{4}$ pies in the space below.

Color the correct number of pie slices to match the given fraction.

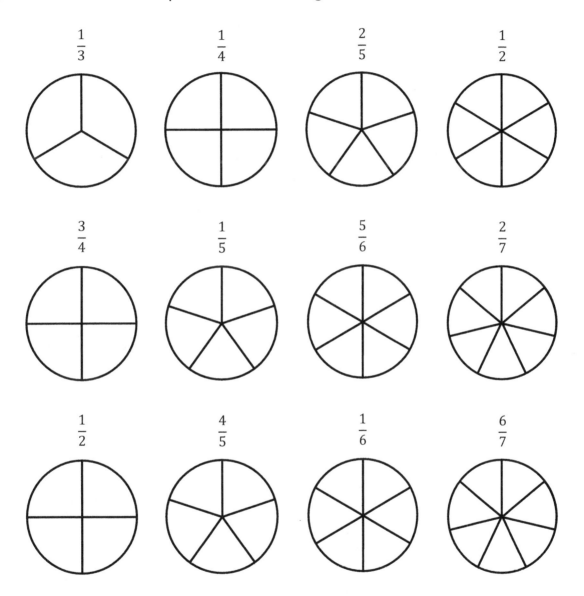

Color the correct number of pie slices to match the given fraction.

$$\frac{3}{5}$$

$$\frac{1}{3}$$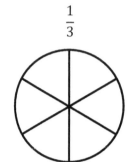

$$\frac{4}{7}$$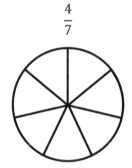

$$\frac{1}{4}$$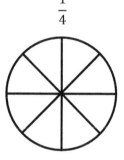

$$\frac{2}{3}$$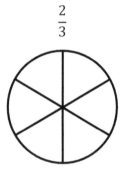

$$\frac{1}{7}$$

$$\frac{1}{8}$$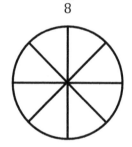

$$\frac{5}{9}$$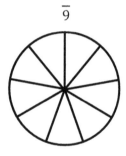

$$\frac{5}{7}$$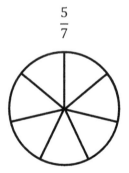

$$\frac{1}{2}$$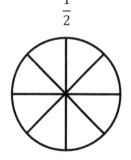

$$\frac{2}{9}$$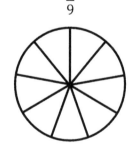

$$\frac{9}{10}$$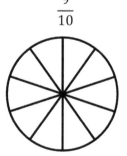

Color the correct number of pie slices to match the given fraction.

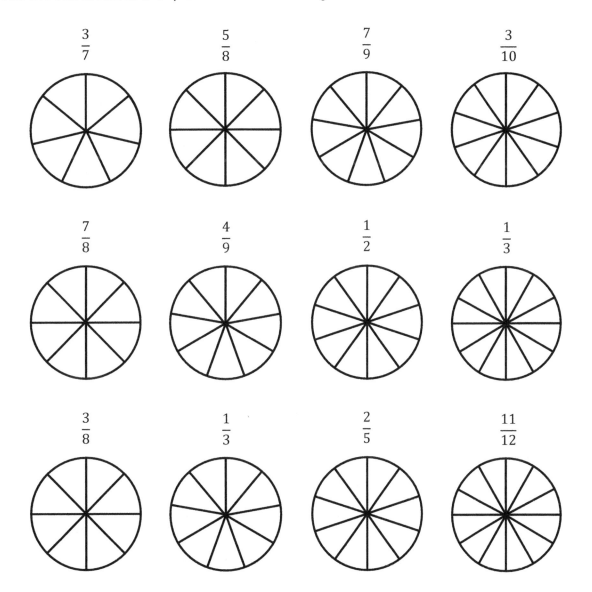

$$\frac{3}{7} \qquad \frac{5}{8} \qquad \frac{7}{9} \qquad \frac{3}{10}$$

$$\frac{7}{8} \qquad \frac{4}{9} \qquad \frac{1}{2} \qquad \frac{1}{3}$$

$$\frac{3}{8} \qquad \frac{1}{3} \qquad \frac{2}{5} \qquad \frac{11}{12}$$

Color the correct number of pie slices to match the given fraction.

$\dfrac{3}{4}$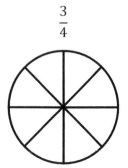

$\dfrac{4}{9}$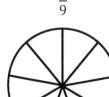

$\dfrac{1}{10}$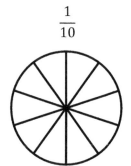

$\dfrac{1}{2}$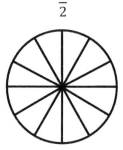

$\dfrac{1}{9}$

$\dfrac{2}{3}$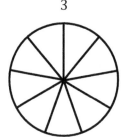

$\dfrac{4}{5}$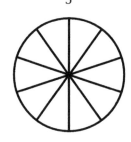

$\dfrac{3}{4}$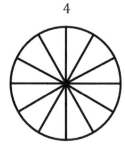

$\dfrac{1}{5}$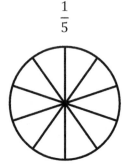

$\dfrac{3}{5}$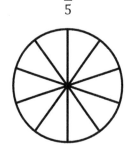

$\dfrac{5}{12}$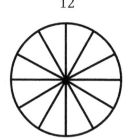

$\dfrac{2}{3}$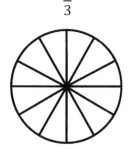

Draw $1\frac{1}{2}$ pies in the space below.

Draw $1\frac{3}{4}$ pies in the space below.

Draw $2\frac{1}{2}$ pies in the space below.

Draw $2\frac{1}{3}$ pies in the space below.

Draw $3\frac{3}{4}$ pies in the space below.

Draw $1\frac{2}{3}$ pies in the space below.

Draw $4\frac{1}{4}$ pies in the space below.

Draw $2\frac{2}{3}$ pies in the space below.

Draw $3\frac{1}{4}$ pies in the space below.

Draw $1\frac{1}{3}$ pies in the space below.

Draw $4\frac{1}{2}$ pies in the space below.

Draw $1\frac{1}{6}$ pies in the space below.

Draw $2\frac{3}{8}$ pies in the space below.

Draw $3\frac{2}{3}$ pies in the space below.

Draw $1\frac{1}{4}$ pies in the space below.

Draw $1\frac{5}{6}$ pies in the space below.

Draw $3\frac{1}{2}$ pies in the space below.

Draw $4\frac{3}{4}$ pies in the space below.

Draw $2\frac{5}{8}$ pies in the space below.

Draw $3\frac{1}{6}$ pies in the space below.

Draw $5\frac{1}{2}$ pies in the space below.

Draw $4\frac{7}{8}$ pies in the space below.

Draw $1\frac{1}{8}$ pies in the space below.

Draw $5\frac{2}{3}$ pies in the space below.

Draw $3\frac{5}{6}$ pies in the space below.

3 Converting Mixed Numbers into Improper Fractions

Basic Concepts: A fraction can be expressed in the following form:

$$\text{fraction} = \frac{\text{numerator}}{\text{denominator}}$$

For example, in the fraction $\frac{3}{4}$, the **numerator** is 3 and the **denominator** is 4. A fraction is called a **proper fraction** if the numerator is less than the denominator. For example, $\frac{1}{2}, \frac{3}{5}$, and $\frac{8}{9}$ are all proper fractions. A fraction is called an **improper fraction** if the numerator is greater than the denominator. For example, $\frac{4}{3}, \frac{5}{2}$, and $\frac{9}{8}$ are all improper fractions.

An improper fraction can alternatively be expressed as a **mixed number**, which includes an integer together with a proper fraction. For example, the mixed number $1\frac{1}{2}$ means one plus one-half, which is equivalent to the improper fraction $\frac{3}{2}$.

A mixed number, like $3\frac{1}{4}$, can be converted into an improper fraction. Multiply the denominator (in this case, 4) times the whole number (in this case, 3) and add the numerator (in this case, 1): $4 \times 3 + 1 = 13$. This is the numerator of the improper fraction. The improper fraction and mixed number have the same denominator. So $3\frac{1}{4}$ is equivalent to $\frac{13}{4}$.

Directions: Convert the given mixed number into an improper fraction as described above. Study the examples below before you begin. Check your answers in the back of the book.

Examples.

$$4\frac{1}{2} = \frac{2 \times 4 + 1}{2} = \frac{9}{2}$$

$$5\frac{3}{8} = \frac{8 \times 5 + 3}{8} = \frac{43}{8}$$

$$2\frac{4}{5} = \frac{5 \times 2 + 4}{5} = \frac{14}{5}$$

$$1\frac{2}{3} = \frac{3 \times 1 + 2}{3} = \frac{5}{3}$$

$7\frac{1}{3}$ $4\frac{2}{3}$ $7\frac{3}{4}$ $8\frac{8}{9}$

$7\frac{3}{8}$ $3\frac{1}{2}$ $1\frac{1}{4}$ $5\frac{2}{9}$

$9\frac{3}{7}$ $7\frac{2}{5}$ $1\frac{7}{8}$ $1\frac{4}{5}$

$7\frac{5}{7}$ $5\frac{3}{5}$ $7\frac{1}{8}$ $6\frac{1}{2}$

$4\frac{1}{2}$ $3\frac{1}{3}$ $2\frac{5}{6}$ $6\frac{2}{9}$

$5\frac{5}{7}$ $\qquad$ $3\frac{1}{2}$ $\qquad$ $3\frac{2}{5}$ $\qquad$ $2\frac{1}{2}$

$2\frac{7}{9}$ $\qquad$ $9\frac{1}{6}$ $\qquad$ $6\frac{5}{6}$ $\qquad$ $6\frac{1}{2}$

$8\frac{3}{4}$ $\qquad$ $9\frac{1}{2}$ $\qquad$ $3\frac{1}{6}$ $\qquad$ $8\frac{1}{8}$

$6\frac{4}{5}$ $\qquad$ $9\frac{3}{8}$ $\qquad$ $4\frac{3}{8}$ $\qquad$ $1\frac{6}{7}$

$8\frac{3}{8}$ $\qquad$ $8\frac{1}{2}$ $\qquad$ $3\frac{1}{6}$ $\qquad$ $2\frac{5}{6}$

$8\frac{1}{2}$ $3\frac{3}{4}$ $3\frac{2}{5}$ $2\frac{2}{3}$

$2\frac{3}{4}$ $3\frac{2}{3}$ $6\frac{4}{7}$ $4\frac{5}{9}$

$4\frac{1}{9}$ $6\frac{1}{2}$ $7\frac{1}{5}$ $9\frac{4}{9}$

$9\frac{1}{4}$ $6\frac{4}{7}$ $2\frac{2}{3}$ $9\frac{5}{8}$

$1\frac{1}{2}$ $1\frac{1}{7}$ $5\frac{2}{5}$ $3\frac{2}{9}$

$3\frac{1}{3}$ $5\frac{5}{8}$ $8\frac{2}{3}$ $6\frac{1}{2}$

$2\frac{2}{3}$ $8\frac{6}{7}$ $3\frac{1}{6}$ $6\frac{7}{9}$

$7\frac{3}{4}$ $2\frac{3}{8}$ $2\frac{3}{4}$ $3\frac{3}{4}$

$8\frac{1}{4}$ $4\frac{3}{5}$ $9\frac{3}{7}$ $1\frac{6}{7}$

$8\frac{1}{2}$ $6\frac{3}{4}$ $3\frac{2}{3}$ $7\frac{5}{6}$

$7\frac{1}{4}$ $2\frac{1}{2}$ $6\frac{2}{3}$ $1\frac{3}{4}$

$1\frac{7}{8}$ $5\frac{2}{3}$ $7\frac{1}{6}$ $7\frac{4}{5}$

$1\frac{2}{5}$ $4\frac{2}{3}$ $5\frac{4}{5}$ $7\frac{3}{4}$

$2\frac{2}{3}$ $1\frac{3}{4}$ $6\frac{3}{7}$ $5\frac{1}{8}$

$3\frac{1}{7}$ $7\frac{1}{2}$ $8\frac{1}{2}$ $9\frac{8}{9}$

$3\frac{1}{4}$ $8\frac{7}{8}$ $2\frac{3}{8}$ $8\frac{6}{7}$

$1\frac{1}{2}$ $1\frac{4}{9}$ $9\frac{3}{8}$ $1\frac{1}{8}$

$6\frac{3}{7}$ $5\frac{7}{8}$ $8\frac{2}{3}$ $3\frac{3}{5}$

$1\frac{8}{9}$ $1\frac{1}{7}$ $4\frac{5}{6}$ $3\frac{5}{6}$

$3\frac{3}{4}$ $4\frac{1}{4}$ $4\frac{1}{8}$ $5\frac{3}{4}$

$$7 \frac{7}{9} \qquad 2 \frac{3}{7} \qquad 7 \frac{4}{5} \qquad 2 \frac{1}{2}$$

$$5 \frac{1}{2} \qquad 5 \frac{1}{5} \qquad 4 \frac{6}{7} \qquad 7 \frac{2}{3}$$

$$4 \frac{7}{8} \qquad 6 \frac{7}{8} \qquad 5 \frac{3}{7} \qquad 8 \frac{7}{9}$$

$$8 \frac{1}{9} \qquad 8 \frac{5}{6} \qquad 7 \frac{1}{5} \qquad 2 \frac{7}{9}$$

$$8 \frac{2}{9} \qquad 6 \frac{4}{5} \qquad 9 \frac{1}{2} \qquad 6 \frac{2}{7}$$

$7\frac{1}{8}$ $1\frac{1}{6}$ $8\frac{1}{9}$ $4\frac{8}{9}$

$4\frac{3}{7}$ $3\frac{2}{5}$ $9\frac{1}{2}$ $1\frac{5}{8}$

$9\frac{1}{2}$ $2\frac{1}{3}$ $6\frac{5}{6}$ $1\frac{1}{4}$

$2\frac{5}{6}$ $2\frac{1}{4}$ $1\frac{7}{8}$ $9\frac{1}{2}$

$1\frac{1}{2}$ $1\frac{1}{6}$ $1\frac{2}{3}$ $1\frac{1}{4}$

$3\frac{5}{8}$　　　$7\frac{4}{5}$　　　$1\frac{7}{9}$　　　$7\frac{1}{6}$

$2\frac{2}{7}$　　　$5\frac{1}{6}$　　　$8\frac{1}{2}$　　　$8\frac{2}{3}$

$4\frac{3}{4}$　　　$7\frac{1}{6}$　　　$2\frac{8}{9}$　　　$7\frac{5}{7}$

$4\frac{1}{2}$　　　$8\frac{2}{9}$　　　$2\frac{7}{9}$　　　$1\frac{1}{8}$

$2\frac{1}{8}$　　　$8\frac{7}{9}$　　　$3\frac{1}{2}$　　　$6\frac{7}{9}$

$9\frac{2}{3}$ $1\frac{8}{9}$ $5\frac{5}{8}$ $5\frac{2}{3}$

$9\frac{1}{2}$ $5\frac{1}{5}$ $2\frac{1}{2}$ $9\frac{1}{2}$

$4\frac{1}{7}$ $6\frac{1}{6}$ $7\frac{1}{2}$ $5\frac{3}{5}$

$2\frac{8}{9}$ $6\frac{1}{8}$ $7\frac{3}{4}$ $5\frac{7}{9}$

$6\frac{2}{3}$ $2\frac{5}{6}$ $9\frac{5}{7}$ $1\frac{1}{2}$

$8\frac{2}{7}$ $3\frac{1}{4}$ $4\frac{1}{3}$ $3\frac{1}{3}$

$7\frac{1}{8}$ $2\frac{4}{9}$ $7\frac{5}{9}$ $3\frac{2}{3}$

$8\frac{5}{8}$ $1\frac{4}{5}$ $8\frac{1}{5}$ $6\frac{4}{5}$

$4\frac{2}{5}$ $7\frac{5}{8}$ $4\frac{2}{7}$ $6\frac{3}{4}$

$5\frac{1}{3}$ $3\frac{5}{6}$ $5\frac{1}{8}$ $2\frac{3}{4}$

4 Converting Improper Fractions into Mixed Numbers

Basic Concepts: To convert an improper fraction, like $\frac{13}{4}$, into a mixed number, divide the numerator (in this case, 13) by the denominator (in this case, 4). The result of the division – called the **quotient** – includes an integer part and a **remainder**. The integer part is the whole number of the mixed number and the remainder is the numerator. The mixed number has the same denominator. In this example, $13 \div 4 = 3R1$. That is, 13 divided by 4 equals 3 with a remainder of 1. Therefore, $\frac{13}{4}$ is equivalent to $3\frac{1}{4}$.

Directions: Convert the improper fraction into a mixed number as described above. Study the examples below before you begin. Check your answers in the back of the book.

Examples.

$$\frac{9}{2} = 9 \div 2 = 4R1 = 4\frac{1}{2}$$

$$\frac{14}{5} = 14 \div 5 = 2R4 = 2\frac{4}{5}$$

$$\frac{43}{8} = 43 \div 8 = 5R3 = 5\frac{3}{8}$$

$$\frac{4}{3} = 4 \div 3 = 1R1 = 1\frac{1}{3}$$

$$\frac{39}{7} = 39 \div 7 = 5R4 = 5\frac{4}{7}$$

For example, in $39 \div 7$, we are asking for the largest whole number that 7 evenly divides into that is less than 39. The answer is 35, which is 7×5. This leaves a remainder of 4. Therefore, $\frac{39}{7}$ equates to $5\frac{4}{7}$ because $39 \div 7$ equals 5 with a remainder of 4.

$$\frac{14}{3} \qquad \frac{35}{4} \qquad \frac{73}{8} \qquad \frac{29}{6}$$

$$\frac{23}{6} \qquad \frac{28}{9} \qquad \frac{77}{9} \qquad \frac{11}{6}$$

$$\frac{15}{4} \qquad \frac{35}{6} \qquad \frac{52}{9} \qquad \frac{53}{6}$$

$$\frac{16}{9} \qquad \frac{12}{5} \qquad \frac{67}{8} \qquad \frac{79}{8}$$

$$\frac{8}{3} \qquad \frac{5}{3} \qquad \frac{41}{5} \qquad \frac{11}{2}$$

$$\frac{41}{6} \qquad \frac{47}{9} \qquad \frac{11}{7} \qquad \frac{22}{7}$$

$$\frac{43}{9} \qquad \frac{3}{2} \qquad \frac{57}{8} \qquad \frac{47}{6}$$

$$\frac{25}{6} \qquad \frac{32}{9} \qquad \frac{47}{9} \qquad \frac{17}{3}$$

$$\frac{8}{7} \qquad \frac{7}{6} \qquad \frac{43}{7} \qquad \frac{10}{3}$$

$$\frac{82}{9} \qquad \frac{51}{7} \qquad \frac{32}{5} \qquad \frac{12}{5}$$

$$\frac{57}{8} \qquad \frac{36}{5} \qquad \frac{66}{7} \qquad \frac{19}{6}$$

$$\frac{43}{6} \qquad \frac{33}{4} \qquad \frac{8}{3} \qquad \frac{17}{3}$$

$$\frac{62}{9} \qquad \frac{59}{8} \qquad \frac{49}{8} \qquad \frac{15}{4}$$

$$\frac{48}{5} \qquad \frac{17}{6} \qquad \frac{5}{3} \qquad \frac{43}{9}$$

$$\frac{23}{9} \qquad \frac{23}{3} \qquad \frac{15}{4} \qquad \frac{39}{7}$$

$$\frac{23}{8} \qquad \frac{68}{9} \qquad \frac{9}{2} \qquad \frac{24}{7}$$

$$\frac{11}{6} \qquad \frac{73}{8} \qquad \frac{29}{8} \qquad \frac{63}{8}$$

$$\frac{16}{5} \qquad \frac{13}{2} \qquad \frac{22}{5} \qquad \frac{29}{4}$$

$$\frac{29}{4} \qquad \frac{34}{5} \qquad \frac{13}{3} \qquad \frac{11}{2}$$

$$\frac{34}{7} \qquad \frac{21}{5} \qquad \frac{37}{8} \qquad \frac{53}{9}$$

$$\frac{15}{2} \qquad \frac{11}{2} \qquad \frac{75}{8} \qquad \frac{24}{5}$$

$$\frac{17}{4} \qquad \frac{16}{3} \qquad \frac{47}{6} \qquad \frac{73}{8}$$

$$\frac{22}{9} \qquad \frac{37}{4} \qquad \frac{16}{3} \qquad \frac{22}{9}$$

$$\frac{19}{2} \qquad \frac{74}{9} \qquad \frac{37}{6} \qquad \frac{19}{9}$$

$$\frac{25}{4} \qquad \frac{35}{4} \qquad \frac{23}{7} \qquad \frac{31}{8}$$

$$\frac{8}{3} \qquad \frac{59}{9} \qquad \frac{57}{7} \qquad \frac{53}{6}$$

$$\frac{83}{9} \qquad \frac{17}{2} \qquad \frac{20}{3} \qquad \frac{9}{2}$$

$$\frac{8}{7} \qquad \frac{29}{7} \qquad \frac{19}{2} \qquad \frac{13}{6}$$

$$\frac{27}{7} \qquad \frac{26}{3} \qquad \frac{17}{6} \qquad \frac{69}{7}$$

$$\frac{73}{8} \qquad \frac{28}{3} \qquad \frac{29}{6} \qquad \frac{13}{2}$$

$$\frac{22}{9} \qquad \frac{11}{7} \qquad \frac{82}{9} \qquad \frac{29}{3}$$

$$\frac{38}{5} \qquad \frac{9}{4} \qquad \frac{17}{9} \qquad \frac{39}{7}$$

$$\frac{22}{3} \qquad \frac{25}{3} \qquad \frac{51}{8} \qquad \frac{9}{4}$$

$$\frac{7}{2} \qquad \frac{23}{3} \qquad \frac{17}{4} \qquad \frac{55}{6}$$

$$\frac{40}{7} \qquad \frac{13}{2} \qquad \frac{19}{2} \qquad \frac{64}{7}$$

$\dfrac{19}{2}$ $\qquad$ $\dfrac{13}{2}$ $\qquad$ $\dfrac{25}{3}$ $\qquad$ $\dfrac{47}{5}$

$\dfrac{25}{7}$ $\qquad$ $\dfrac{54}{7}$ $\qquad$ $\dfrac{25}{4}$ $\qquad$ $\dfrac{38}{7}$

$\dfrac{71}{8}$ $\qquad$ $\dfrac{11}{6}$ $\qquad$ $\dfrac{11}{8}$ $\qquad$ $\dfrac{27}{5}$

$\dfrac{22}{3}$ $\qquad$ $\dfrac{18}{5}$ $\qquad$ $\dfrac{17}{6}$ $\qquad$ $\dfrac{25}{3}$

$\dfrac{31}{6}$ $\qquad$ $\dfrac{55}{9}$ $\qquad$ $\dfrac{8}{3}$ $\qquad$ $\dfrac{11}{6}$

$$\frac{58}{9} \qquad \frac{39}{8} \qquad \frac{11}{4} \qquad \frac{11}{3}$$

$$\frac{57}{8} \qquad \frac{22}{5} \qquad \frac{49}{5} \qquad \frac{13}{2}$$

$$\frac{3}{2} \qquad \frac{40}{7} \qquad \frac{19}{7} \qquad \frac{35}{8}$$

$$\frac{89}{9} \qquad \frac{13}{5} \qquad \frac{19}{2} \qquad \frac{17}{2}$$

$$\frac{15}{2} \qquad \frac{65}{9} \qquad \frac{27}{5} \qquad \frac{19}{9}$$

$$\frac{41}{6} \qquad \frac{26}{3} \qquad \frac{43}{8} \qquad \frac{43}{5}$$

$$\frac{59}{8} \qquad \frac{13}{4} \qquad \frac{22}{3} \qquad \frac{11}{2}$$

$$\frac{23}{6} \qquad \frac{23}{3} \qquad \frac{27}{8} \qquad \frac{29}{6}$$

$$\frac{46}{9} \qquad \frac{26}{9} \qquad \frac{14}{9} \qquad \frac{22}{9}$$

$$\frac{15}{2} \qquad \frac{27}{4} \qquad \frac{66}{7} \qquad \frac{53}{7}$$

$$\frac{53}{6} \qquad \frac{49}{5} \qquad \frac{88}{9} \qquad \frac{10}{3}$$

$$\frac{36}{5} \qquad \frac{31}{6} \qquad \frac{20}{9} \qquad \frac{67}{9}$$

$$\frac{5}{3} \qquad \frac{19}{7} \qquad \frac{55}{6} \qquad \frac{25}{4}$$

$$\frac{31}{6} \qquad \frac{17}{4} \qquad \frac{77}{8} \qquad \frac{23}{4}$$

$$\frac{41}{6} \qquad \frac{53}{6} \qquad \frac{20}{3} \qquad \frac{6}{5}$$

5 Reducing Fractions and Mixed Numbers

Basic Concepts: When two or more numbers are multiplied together, the numbers being multiplied are called **factors**. For example, in $6 \times 2 = 12$, the 6 and 2 are called factors. Note that 12 can also be factored as $4 \times 3 = 12$. In this case, the 4 and 3 are factors. The **prime factors** of 12 are 2, 2, and 3 since $2 \times 2 \times 3 = 12$.

A pair of numbers, like 12 and 18, may share **common factors**. For example, 12 and 18 are both divisible by 3, so 3 is a common factor of 12 and 18. The **greatest common factor** of 12 and 18 is 6 because 6 is the largest number that evenly divides into both 12 and 18.

A fraction, like $\frac{12}{18}$, can be reduced when the numerator and denominator share a common factor. The **reduced fraction** is obtained by dividing both the numerator and denominator by the greatest common factor. The fraction $\frac{12}{18}$ is reduced by dividing 12 by 6 and dividing 18 by 6 (since 6 is the greatest common factor of 12 and 18). Therefore, $\frac{12}{18} = \frac{12 \div 6}{18 \div 6} = \frac{2}{3}$. Whenever you solve a math problem and obtain an answer that is a fraction, you should always express your answer as a reduced fraction. (The underlying idea is that if you divide the numerator and denominator of a fraction by the same factor, you obtain an equivalent fraction.)

A mixed number can be reduced in the same way, leaving the whole number alone and reducing just the proper fraction. For example, in $2\frac{6}{8}$, the $\frac{6}{8}$ can be reduced. The greatest common factor of 6 and 8 is 2. Therefore, $\frac{6}{8} = \frac{6 \div 2}{8 \div 2} = \frac{3}{4}$, so $2\frac{6}{8}$ reduces to $2\frac{3}{4}$.

Directions: Reduce the given fraction or mixed number as described above. Study the examples below before you begin. Check your answers in the back of the book.

Examples.

$$\frac{16}{12} = \frac{16 \div 4}{12 \div 4} = \frac{4}{3} \quad , \quad \frac{15}{25} = \frac{15 \div 5}{25 \div 5} = \frac{3}{5}$$

$$\frac{4}{24} = \frac{4 \div 4}{24 \div 4} = \frac{1}{6} \quad , \quad \frac{10}{5} = \frac{10 \div 5}{5 \div 5} = \frac{2}{1} = 2$$

$$3\frac{16}{24} = 3\frac{16 \div 8}{24 \div 8} = 3\frac{2}{3} \quad , \quad 1\frac{6}{9} = 1\frac{6 \div 3}{9 \div 3} = 1\frac{2}{3}$$

$\dfrac{6}{18}$ $\qquad$ $9\,\dfrac{27}{45}$ $\qquad$ $\dfrac{21}{28}$ $\qquad$ $3\,\dfrac{36}{48}$

$7\,\dfrac{9}{24}$ $\qquad$ $\dfrac{22}{33}$ $\qquad$ $7\,\dfrac{22}{55}$ $\qquad$ $\dfrac{45}{10}$

$\dfrac{18}{45}$ $\qquad$ $7\,\dfrac{14}{18}$ $\qquad$ $\dfrac{18}{48}$ $\qquad$ $6\,\dfrac{27}{36}$

$9\,\dfrac{2}{6}$ $\qquad$ $\dfrac{55}{33}$ $\qquad$ $6\,\dfrac{36}{42}$ $\qquad$ $\dfrac{4}{20}$

$\dfrac{88}{99}$ $\qquad$ $3\,\dfrac{11}{99}$ $\qquad$ $\dfrac{21}{35}$ $\qquad$ $2\,\dfrac{21}{27}$

$1 \dfrac{63}{81}$ $\dfrac{21}{27}$ $9 \dfrac{44}{77}$ $\dfrac{50}{40}$

$\dfrac{54}{30}$ $1 \dfrac{10}{20}$ $\dfrac{12}{108}$ $9 \dfrac{12}{24}$

$4 \dfrac{12}{15}$ $\dfrac{108}{96}$ $2 \dfrac{40}{48}$ $\dfrac{3}{9}$

$\dfrac{12}{60}$ $6 \dfrac{20}{50}$ $\dfrac{49}{14}$ $7 \dfrac{6}{9}$

$4 \dfrac{20}{30}$ $\dfrac{16}{28}$ $5 \dfrac{20}{32}$ $\dfrac{9}{15}$

$\frac{10}{90}$　　　　$8\,\frac{35}{56}$　　　　$\frac{9}{12}$　　　　$3\,\frac{33}{44}$

$9\,\frac{25}{40}$　　　　$\frac{18}{42}$　　　　$9\,\frac{25}{30}$　　　　$\frac{8}{28}$

$\frac{3}{6}$　　　　$1\,\frac{4}{10}$　　　　$\frac{6}{48}$　　　　$5\,\frac{9}{36}$

$5\,\frac{24}{36}$　　　　$\frac{33}{88}$　　　　$2\,\frac{10}{25}$　　　　$\frac{36}{96}$

$\frac{4}{6}$　　　　$4\,\frac{10}{70}$　　　　$\frac{10}{8}$　　　　$5\,\frac{45}{81}$

$8 \dfrac{2}{8}$ $\qquad$ $\dfrac{10}{60}$ $\qquad$ $7 \dfrac{33}{44}$ $\qquad$ $\dfrac{18}{24}$

$\dfrac{64}{40}$ $\qquad$ $4 \dfrac{10}{30}$ $\qquad$ $\dfrac{21}{27}$ $\qquad$ $2 \dfrac{2}{6}$

$6 \dfrac{7}{42}$ $\qquad$ $\dfrac{20}{16}$ $\qquad$ $1 \dfrac{9}{18}$ $\qquad$ $\dfrac{12}{54}$

$\dfrac{33}{22}$ $\qquad$ $7 \dfrac{3}{12}$ $\qquad$ $\dfrac{45}{40}$ $\qquad$ $4 \dfrac{50}{80}$

$5 \dfrac{10}{12}$ $\qquad$ $\dfrac{15}{10}$ $\qquad$ $5 \dfrac{10}{16}$ $\qquad$ $\dfrac{35}{63}$

$\dfrac{8}{14}$ $2\,\dfrac{2}{4}$ $\dfrac{70}{20}$ $6\,\dfrac{3}{12}$

$9\,\dfrac{9}{36}$ $\dfrac{30}{18}$ $6\,\dfrac{24}{64}$ $\dfrac{9}{6}$

$\dfrac{63}{28}$ $1\,\dfrac{44}{55}$ $\dfrac{42}{30}$ $8\,\dfrac{8}{40}$

$2\,\dfrac{18}{27}$ $\dfrac{156}{84}$ $7\,\dfrac{9}{63}$ $\dfrac{42}{54}$

$\dfrac{6}{24}$ $3\,\dfrac{36}{60}$ $\dfrac{49}{28}$ $7\,\dfrac{48}{84}$

$1\dfrac{18}{48}$ $\dfrac{8}{40}$ $6\dfrac{9}{21}$ $\dfrac{99}{88}$

$\dfrac{36}{63}$ $4\dfrac{30}{36}$ $\dfrac{60}{96}$ $4\dfrac{12}{18}$

$4\dfrac{12}{24}$ $\dfrac{99}{44}$ $6\dfrac{70}{90}$ $\dfrac{45}{18}$

$\dfrac{60}{24}$ $5\dfrac{24}{60}$ $\dfrac{117}{63}$ $4\dfrac{64}{72}$

$9\dfrac{16}{28}$ $\dfrac{81}{72}$ $9\dfrac{4}{24}$ $\dfrac{36}{21}$

$\dfrac{15}{6}$　　　　$9\,\dfrac{12}{27}$　　　　$\dfrac{4}{28}$　　　　$5\,\dfrac{2}{4}$

$8\,\dfrac{3}{9}$　　　　$\dfrac{70}{30}$　　　　$9\,\dfrac{30}{48}$　　　　$\dfrac{40}{25}$

$\dfrac{36}{30}$　　　　$7\,\dfrac{2}{4}$　　　　$\dfrac{20}{12}$　　　　$4\,\dfrac{70}{90}$

$6\,\dfrac{10}{60}$　　　　$\dfrac{55}{44}$　　　　$8\,\dfrac{18}{27}$　　　　$\dfrac{20}{24}$

$\dfrac{35}{40}$　　　　$4\,\dfrac{27}{63}$　　　　$\dfrac{72}{56}$　　　　$9\,\dfrac{2}{14}$

$8\frac{8}{18}$ $\frac{60}{48}$ $7\frac{56}{64}$ $\frac{48}{30}$

$\frac{36}{45}$ $7\frac{11}{66}$ $\frac{7}{35}$ $3\frac{24}{56}$

$8\frac{6}{9}$ $\frac{56}{64}$ $3\frac{36}{63}$ $\frac{80}{50}$

$\frac{6}{16}$ $5\frac{12}{21}$ $\frac{49}{28}$ $7\frac{3}{21}$

$4\frac{27}{63}$ $\frac{117}{63}$ $7\frac{10}{50}$ $\frac{77}{66}$

$\dfrac{2}{6}$

$1\,\dfrac{2}{8}$

$\dfrac{7}{63}$

$3\,\dfrac{7}{49}$

$6\,\dfrac{18}{48}$

$\dfrac{12}{42}$

$9\,\dfrac{10}{15}$

$\dfrac{49}{42}$

$\dfrac{50}{20}$

$1\,\dfrac{11}{44}$

$\dfrac{49}{42}$

$8\,\dfrac{56}{64}$

$2\,\dfrac{10}{30}$

$\dfrac{4}{16}$

$6\,\dfrac{12}{84}$

$\dfrac{6}{18}$

$\dfrac{60}{35}$

$9\,\dfrac{11}{77}$

$\dfrac{6}{10}$

$6\,\dfrac{30}{35}$

$3 \frac{72}{81}$ $\qquad$ $\frac{72}{27}$ $\qquad$ $2 \frac{7}{14}$ $\qquad$ $\frac{56}{49}$

$\frac{5}{15}$ $\qquad$ $3 \frac{12}{48}$ $\qquad$ $\frac{14}{6}$ $\qquad$ $4 \frac{9}{18}$

$9 \frac{15}{24}$ $\qquad$ $\frac{108}{96}$ $\qquad$ $7 \frac{2}{10}$ $\qquad$ $\frac{60}{24}$

$\frac{10}{50}$ $\qquad$ $1 \frac{12}{16}$ $\qquad$ $\frac{2}{8}$ $\qquad$ $6 \frac{21}{49}$

$1 \frac{12}{15}$ $\qquad$ $\frac{40}{72}$ $\qquad$ $8 \frac{8}{48}$ $\qquad$ $\frac{25}{45}$

$\dfrac{72}{32}$ $2\dfrac{25}{45}$ $\dfrac{30}{20}$ $4\dfrac{11}{22}$

$5\dfrac{55}{66}$ $\dfrac{80}{90}$ $6\dfrac{7}{21}$ $\dfrac{10}{15}$

$\dfrac{10}{14}$ $8\dfrac{9}{36}$ $\dfrac{45}{25}$ $2\dfrac{9}{18}$

$3\dfrac{6}{42}$ $\dfrac{21}{12}$ $2\dfrac{7}{42}$ $\dfrac{21}{28}$

$\dfrac{24}{30}$ $1\dfrac{5}{30}$ $\dfrac{20}{30}$ $5\dfrac{30}{42}$

6 Finding Lowest Common Denominators

Basic Concepts: Given two proper or improper fractions, like $\frac{5}{6}$ and $\frac{7}{4}$, it is sometimes necessary to find a **common denominator**. One way to find a common denominator is by multiplying the denominators together – in this case, that would be $6 \times 4 = 24$. However, it is often better to find the **lowest common denominator**. The lowest common denominator is the smallest whole number that is a multiple of both of the denominators. For $\frac{5}{6}$ and $\frac{7}{4}$, the two denominators are 6 and 4. The smallest whole number that is a multiple of both 6 and 4 is 12: $6 \times 2 = 12$ and $4 \times 3 = 12$. Therefore, the lowest common denominator for $\frac{5}{6}$ and $\frac{7}{4}$ is 12.

Tip: In this chapter, you can ignore the numerators of the given fractions.

Directions: For each pair of fractions given, determine the lowest common denominator as described above. Study the examples below before you begin. Check your answers in the back of the book.

Example 1. $\frac{1}{3}$ and $\frac{3}{4}$. The smallest whole number that is a multiple of 3 and 4 is 12: $3 \times 4 = 12$ and $4 \times 3 = 12$. Therefore, the lowest common denominator is 12.

Example 2. $\frac{3}{8}$ and $\frac{5}{6}$. The smallest whole number that is a multiple of 8 and 6 is 24: $8 \times 3 = 24$ and $6 \times 4 = 24$. Therefore, the lowest common denominator is 24. (Note that 48 could also be a common denominator, but 24 is the lowest common denominator.)

Example 3. $\frac{1}{6}$ and $\frac{4}{9}$. The smallest whole number that is a multiple of 6 and 9 is 18: $6 \times 3 = 18$ and $9 \times 2 = 18$. Therefore, the lowest common denominator is 18. (Note that 54 could also be a common denominator, but 18 is the lowest common denominator.)

Example 4. $\frac{18}{5}$ and $\frac{3}{5}$. The smallest whole number that is a multiple of 5 and 5 is 5: Therefore, the lowest common denominator is 5. When the two denominators are the same, that will be the lowest common denominator.

$\dfrac{2}{5}$ and $\dfrac{3}{2}$ $\dfrac{9}{4}$ and $\dfrac{5}{8}$ $\dfrac{11}{6}$ and $\dfrac{10}{9}$

$\dfrac{13}{4}$ and $\dfrac{7}{3}$ $\dfrac{1}{2}$ and $\dfrac{3}{8}$ $\dfrac{2}{3}$ and $\dfrac{4}{5}$

$\dfrac{11}{6}$ and $\dfrac{11}{4}$ $\dfrac{10}{7}$ and $\dfrac{13}{6}$ $\dfrac{8}{3}$ and $\dfrac{5}{2}$

$\dfrac{7}{4}$ and $\dfrac{15}{7}$ $\dfrac{1}{8}$ and $\dfrac{1}{6}$ $\dfrac{11}{8}$ and $\dfrac{5}{9}$

$\dfrac{3}{10}$ and $\dfrac{17}{15}$ $\dfrac{15}{8}$ and $\dfrac{6}{5}$ $\dfrac{4}{9}$ and $\dfrac{12}{5}$

$\dfrac{2}{9}$ and $\dfrac{13}{12}$ $\dfrac{5}{6}$ and $\dfrac{2}{3}$ $\dfrac{11}{8}$ and $\dfrac{10}{7}$

$\dfrac{8}{5}$ and $\dfrac{5}{4}$ $\dfrac{3}{7}$ and $\dfrac{3}{2}$ $\dfrac{11}{12}$ and $\dfrac{7}{8}$

$\dfrac{4}{7}$ and $\dfrac{2}{5}$ $\dfrac{5}{16}$ and $\dfrac{17}{12}$ $\dfrac{10}{9}$ and $\dfrac{1}{6}$

$\dfrac{9}{10}$ and $\dfrac{1}{12}$ $\dfrac{2}{3}$ and $\dfrac{10}{7}$ $\dfrac{8}{15}$ and $\dfrac{5}{12}$

$\dfrac{7}{18}$ and $\dfrac{8}{9}$ $\dfrac{7}{6}$ and $\dfrac{3}{10}$ $\dfrac{5}{2}$ and $\dfrac{1}{4}$

$\dfrac{19}{12}$ and $\dfrac{31}{20}$ $\dfrac{41}{25}$ and $\dfrac{22}{15}$ $\dfrac{2}{9}$ and $\dfrac{12}{5}$

$\dfrac{11}{4}$ and $\dfrac{9}{10}$ $\dfrac{11}{5}$ and $\dfrac{12}{5}$ $\dfrac{7}{30}$ and $\dfrac{11}{20}$

$\dfrac{8}{11}$ and $\dfrac{4}{3}$ $\dfrac{9}{20}$ and $\dfrac{8}{15}$ $\dfrac{1}{6}$ and $\dfrac{12}{7}$

$\dfrac{35}{18}$ and $\dfrac{7}{12}$ $\dfrac{16}{5}$ and $\dfrac{5}{2}$ $\dfrac{8}{15}$ and $\dfrac{11}{6}$

$\dfrac{8}{21}$ and $\dfrac{15}{14}$ $\dfrac{13}{6}$ and $\dfrac{3}{8}$ $\dfrac{1}{3}$ and $\dfrac{23}{8}$

$\dfrac{8}{9}$ and $\dfrac{11}{6}$ $\qquad$ $\dfrac{3}{16}$ and $\dfrac{5}{24}$ $\qquad$ $\dfrac{25}{8}$ and $\dfrac{22}{7}$

$\dfrac{25}{24}$ and $\dfrac{19}{20}$ $\qquad$ $\dfrac{9}{2}$ and $\dfrac{9}{7}$ $\qquad$ $\dfrac{16}{25}$ and $\dfrac{7}{20}$

$\dfrac{3}{4}$ and $\dfrac{21}{10}$ $\qquad$ $\dfrac{17}{6}$ and $\dfrac{4}{15}$ $\qquad$ $\dfrac{4}{7}$ and $\dfrac{9}{14}$

$\dfrac{16}{21}$ and $\dfrac{19}{6}$ $\qquad$ $\dfrac{11}{10}$ and $\dfrac{11}{18}$ $\qquad$ $\dfrac{4}{15}$ and $\dfrac{1}{10}$

$\dfrac{17}{20}$ and $\dfrac{14}{5}$ $\qquad$ $\dfrac{23}{20}$ and $\dfrac{21}{8}$ $\qquad$ $\dfrac{5}{24}$ and $\dfrac{1}{12}$

$\dfrac{19}{30}$ and $\dfrac{17}{10}$ $\dfrac{5}{6}$ and $\dfrac{21}{4}$ $\dfrac{20}{3}$ and $\dfrac{11}{2}$

$\dfrac{8}{7}$ and $\dfrac{4}{3}$ $\dfrac{11}{12}$ and $\dfrac{29}{30}$ $\dfrac{27}{8}$ and $\dfrac{19}{12}$

$\dfrac{4}{33}$ and $\dfrac{13}{22}$ $\dfrac{16}{9}$ and $\dfrac{9}{4}$ $\dfrac{23}{30}$ and $\dfrac{23}{18}$

$\dfrac{16}{21}$ and $\dfrac{25}{28}$ $\dfrac{20}{27}$ and $\dfrac{11}{18}$ $\dfrac{29}{7}$ and $\dfrac{15}{8}$

$\dfrac{20}{9}$ and $\dfrac{15}{2}$ $\dfrac{7}{12}$ and $\dfrac{17}{27}$ $\dfrac{25}{8}$ and $\dfrac{13}{6}$

$\dfrac{9}{20}$ and $\dfrac{7}{30}$ $\dfrac{2}{9}$ and $\dfrac{23}{12}$ $\dfrac{24}{7}$ and $\dfrac{3}{7}$

$\dfrac{19}{12}$ and $\dfrac{13}{20}$ $\dfrac{3}{10}$ and $\dfrac{1}{8}$ $\dfrac{27}{12}$ and $\dfrac{19}{8}$

$\dfrac{25}{7}$ and $\dfrac{21}{10}$ $\dfrac{7}{18}$ and $\dfrac{11}{24}$ $\dfrac{14}{9}$ and $\dfrac{5}{3}$

$\dfrac{17}{36}$ and $\dfrac{29}{24}$ $\dfrac{31}{12}$ and $\dfrac{24}{5}$ $\dfrac{39}{35}$ and $\dfrac{17}{14}$

$\dfrac{1}{2}$ and $\dfrac{3}{7}$ $\dfrac{11}{32}$ and $\dfrac{35}{24}$ $\dfrac{13}{4}$ and $\dfrac{19}{10}$

$\dfrac{20}{9}$ and $\dfrac{35}{6}$ $\dfrac{17}{36}$ and $\dfrac{15}{8}$ $\dfrac{35}{16}$ and $\dfrac{29}{12}$

$\dfrac{32}{5}$ and $\dfrac{17}{4}$ $\dfrac{16}{7}$ and $\dfrac{37}{12}$ $\dfrac{7}{24}$ and $\dfrac{23}{10}$

$\dfrac{3}{32}$ and $\dfrac{19}{6}$ $\dfrac{31}{10}$ and $\dfrac{23}{6}$ $\dfrac{5}{34}$ and $\dfrac{35}{4}$

$\dfrac{11}{40}$ and $\dfrac{29}{30}$ $\dfrac{8}{15}$ and $\dfrac{12}{35}$ $\dfrac{8}{3}$ and $\dfrac{34}{5}$

$\dfrac{26}{9}$ and $\dfrac{4}{7}$ $\dfrac{2}{25}$ and $\dfrac{21}{40}$ $\dfrac{5}{24}$ and $\dfrac{37}{40}$

$\dfrac{19}{40}$ and $\dfrac{31}{16}$ $\qquad$ $\dfrac{8}{15}$ and $\dfrac{33}{20}$ $\qquad$ $\dfrac{35}{4}$ and $\dfrac{27}{2}$

$\dfrac{16}{21}$ and $\dfrac{23}{14}$ $\qquad$ $\dfrac{1}{10}$ and $\dfrac{13}{36}$ $\qquad$ $\dfrac{3}{20}$ and $\dfrac{25}{24}$

$\dfrac{22}{15}$ and $\dfrac{31}{40}$ $\qquad$ $\dfrac{7}{30}$ and $\dfrac{25}{8}$ $\qquad$ $\dfrac{15}{8}$ and $\dfrac{18}{5}$

$\dfrac{19}{3}$ and $\dfrac{4}{11}$ $\qquad$ $\dfrac{2}{3}$ and $\dfrac{37}{6}$ $\qquad$ $\dfrac{19}{40}$ and $\dfrac{23}{12}$

$\dfrac{1}{12}$ and $\dfrac{17}{18}$ $\qquad$ $\dfrac{21}{4}$ and $\dfrac{17}{7}$ $\qquad$ $\dfrac{13}{30}$ and $\dfrac{11}{18}$

$\dfrac{25}{42}$ and $\dfrac{33}{28}$ $\dfrac{41}{20}$ and $\dfrac{17}{8}$ $\dfrac{12}{11}$ and $\dfrac{9}{8}$

$\dfrac{23}{45}$ and $\dfrac{43}{20}$ $\dfrac{7}{10}$ and $\dfrac{19}{3}$ $\dfrac{17}{20}$ and $\dfrac{35}{6}$

$\dfrac{29}{3}$ and $\dfrac{27}{8}$ $\dfrac{43}{12}$ and $\dfrac{5}{42}$ $\dfrac{4}{7}$ and $\dfrac{16}{5}$

$\dfrac{25}{4}$ and $\dfrac{28}{5}$ $\dfrac{11}{16}$ and $\dfrac{7}{30}$ $\dfrac{25}{18}$ and $\dfrac{16}{15}$

$\dfrac{45}{44}$ and $\dfrac{25}{33}$ $\dfrac{11}{14}$ and $\dfrac{18}{5}$ $\dfrac{31}{10}$ and $\dfrac{23}{8}$

$\dfrac{47}{48}$ and $\dfrac{41}{32}$ $\dfrac{35}{6}$ and $\dfrac{26}{9}$ $\dfrac{17}{8}$ and $\dfrac{9}{14}$

$\dfrac{11}{50}$ and $\dfrac{29}{20}$ $\dfrac{7}{2}$ and $\dfrac{44}{9}$ $\dfrac{49}{4}$ and $\dfrac{23}{14}$

$\dfrac{37}{12}$ and $\dfrac{5}{12}$ $\dfrac{3}{10}$ and $\dfrac{8}{45}$ $\dfrac{27}{50}$ and $\dfrac{47}{15}$

$\dfrac{35}{6}$ and $\dfrac{11}{12}$ $\dfrac{41}{40}$ and $\dfrac{1}{12}$ $\dfrac{19}{24}$ and $\dfrac{45}{8}$

$\dfrac{19}{36}$ and $\dfrac{19}{24}$ $\dfrac{43}{24}$ and $\dfrac{35}{16}$ $\dfrac{50}{13}$ and $\dfrac{20}{3}$

$\dfrac{3}{8}$ and $\dfrac{8}{3}$ $\dfrac{29}{21}$ and $\dfrac{17}{12}$ $\dfrac{53}{60}$ and $\dfrac{61}{40}$

$\dfrac{59}{36}$ and $\dfrac{4}{27}$ $\dfrac{8}{15}$ and $\dfrac{50}{3}$ $\dfrac{41}{18}$ and $\dfrac{23}{60}$

$\dfrac{1}{6}$ and $\dfrac{16}{15}$ $\dfrac{7}{60}$ and $\dfrac{55}{24}$ $\dfrac{59}{6}$ and $\dfrac{26}{7}$

$\dfrac{9}{56}$ and $\dfrac{9}{16}$ $\dfrac{49}{12}$ and $\dfrac{33}{8}$ $\dfrac{55}{12}$ and $\dfrac{25}{18}$

$\dfrac{1}{4}$ and $\dfrac{1}{3}$ $\dfrac{11}{60}$ and $\dfrac{9}{50}$ $\dfrac{23}{60}$ and $\dfrac{14}{25}$

7 Comparing Fractions

Basic Concepts: Two fractions, like $\frac{5}{6}$ and $\frac{3}{4}$, can be compared by expressing them with a common denominator. For $\frac{5}{6}$ and $\frac{3}{4}$, the lowest common denominator is 12 (as explained in Chapter 6). To express each fraction with the lowest common denominator, multiply the numerator and denominator of each fraction by the factor needed to make the lowest common denominator. For example, multiply both the 5 and 6 of $\frac{5}{6}$ by 2 to make a denominator of 12: $\frac{5}{6} = \frac{5\times2}{6\times2} = \frac{10}{12}$. Similarly, multiply both the 3 and 4 of $\frac{3}{4}$ by 3 to make a denominator of 12: $\frac{3}{4} = \frac{3\times3}{4\times3} = \frac{9}{12}$. Once both fractions are expressed with a common denominator, whichever fraction has the greatest numerator is largest. In this case, $\frac{5}{6} > \frac{3}{4}$ because $\frac{10}{12} > \frac{9}{12}$.

To compare a fraction to an integer, first express the fraction as an integer by dividing it by 1. For example, comparing $\frac{7}{2}$ and 3, first write 3 as $\frac{3}{1}$. The lowest common denominator between $\frac{7}{2}$ and $\frac{3}{1}$ is 2. Now we write $\frac{3}{1} = \frac{3\times2}{1\times2} = \frac{6}{2}$. Since $\frac{7}{2} > \frac{6}{2}$, it follows that $\frac{7}{2} > 3$. To compare a mixed number to a fraction, first convert the mixed number into an improper fraction, following the technique of Chapter 3. (**Note:** $>$ means greater than and $<$ means less than.)

Directions: For each pair of fractions given, express each fraction with the lowest common denominator as described above. Then compare numerators to determine which is larger. Study the examples below before you begin. Check your answers in the back of the book.

Example 1. $\frac{1}{2}$ and $\frac{4}{9}$. The lowest common denominator is 18 (see Chapter 6). Rewrite the two fractions with this common denominator: $\frac{1}{2} = \frac{1\times9}{2\times9} = \frac{9}{18}$ and $\frac{4}{9} = \frac{4\times2}{9\times2} = \frac{8}{18}$. Since $\frac{9}{18} > \frac{8}{18}, \frac{1}{2} > \frac{4}{9}$.

Example 2. $\frac{9}{4}$ and 2. First write $2 = \frac{2}{1}$. The lowest common denominator is 4. Rewrite the two fractions with this common denominator: $\frac{2}{1} = \frac{2\times4}{1\times4} = \frac{8}{4}$. Since $\frac{9}{4} > \frac{8}{4}, \frac{9}{4} > 2$.

Example 3. $\frac{2}{4}$ and $\frac{3}{6}$. The lowest common denominator is 12. Rewrite the two fractions with this common denominator: $\frac{2}{4} = \frac{2\times3}{4\times3} = \frac{6}{12}$ and $\frac{3}{6} = \frac{3\times2}{6\times2} = \frac{6}{12}$. Since both equal $\frac{6}{12}, \frac{2}{4} = \frac{3}{6}$.

Example 3. $2\frac{1}{2}$ and $\frac{8}{3}$. The lowest common denominator is 6. Rewrite the two fractions with this common denominator: $2\frac{1}{2} = \frac{2\times2+1}{2} = \frac{5\times3}{2\times3} = \frac{15}{6}$ and $\frac{8}{3} = \frac{8\times2}{3\times2} = \frac{16}{6}$. Since $\frac{15}{6} < \frac{16}{6}, 2\frac{1}{2} < \frac{8}{3}$.

$\frac{11}{20}$ and $\frac{1}{2}$ $\frac{24}{6}$ and $\frac{22}{2}$ $\frac{17}{2}$ and 8

$1\frac{16}{23}$ and $\frac{13}{8}$ $\frac{8}{13}$ and $\frac{2}{14}$ $\frac{17}{11}$ and $\frac{19}{3}$

1 and $\frac{24}{16}$ $\frac{9}{5}$ and $\frac{16}{14}$ $\frac{2}{4}$ and $\frac{13}{20}$

$\frac{24}{18}$ and $\frac{24}{23}$ $\frac{20}{21}$ and $\frac{8}{14}$ $\frac{23}{22}$ and $1\frac{2}{3}$

$\frac{2}{8}$ and $\frac{13}{20}$ $\frac{19}{6}$ and $\frac{12}{6}$ $\frac{24}{18}$ and 1

8   $\dfrac{3}{7}$ and $\dfrac{24}{3}$ $\dfrac{9}{11}$ and $\dfrac{2}{7}$ $\dfrac{21}{13}$ and $\dfrac{12}{3}$

2   and $\dfrac{17}{10}$ $\dfrac{8}{2}$ and $\dfrac{24}{23}$ $\dfrac{11}{15}$ and $\dfrac{2}{3}$

$\dfrac{20}{19}$ and $\dfrac{17}{12}$ $\dfrac{1}{2}$ and $\dfrac{10}{20}$ $\dfrac{24}{20}$ and $1\dfrac{2}{14}$

$\dfrac{2}{8}$ and $\dfrac{2}{16}$ $\dfrac{24}{23}$ and $\dfrac{16}{7}$ $\dfrac{5}{3}$ and 1

1   $\dfrac{12}{17}$ and $\dfrac{5}{3}$ $\dfrac{1}{3}$ and $\dfrac{14}{15}$ $\dfrac{23}{20}$ and $\dfrac{22}{14}$

2 and $\dfrac{18}{13}$ $\dfrac{15}{4}$ and $\dfrac{21}{16}$ $\dfrac{3}{5}$ and $\dfrac{3}{9}$

$\dfrac{16}{7}$ and $\dfrac{18}{12}$ $\dfrac{2}{9}$ and $\dfrac{8}{10}$ $\dfrac{10}{7}$ and $1\dfrac{9}{14}$

$\dfrac{11}{20}$ and $\dfrac{4}{6}$ $\dfrac{22}{21}$ and $\dfrac{24}{10}$ $\dfrac{17}{5}$ and 4

$4\dfrac{2}{8}$ and $\dfrac{12}{3}$ $\dfrac{9}{12}$ and $\dfrac{10}{17}$ $\dfrac{24}{19}$ and $\dfrac{24}{23}$

2 and $\dfrac{14}{6}$ $\dfrac{24}{19}$ and $\dfrac{17}{14}$ $\dfrac{1}{5}$ and $\dfrac{4}{11}$

$\dfrac{24}{22}$ and $\dfrac{20}{9}$ $\qquad$ $\dfrac{1}{9}$ and $\dfrac{2}{3}$ $\qquad$ $\dfrac{10}{6}$ and $1\dfrac{15}{23}$

$\dfrac{3}{10}$ and $\dfrac{2}{3}$ $\qquad$ $\dfrac{21}{15}$ and $\dfrac{22}{11}$ $\qquad$ $\dfrac{9}{7}$ and 2

$3\,\dfrac{2}{5}$ and $\dfrac{15}{5}$ $\qquad$ $\dfrac{1}{7}$ and $\dfrac{1}{23}$ $\qquad$ $\dfrac{13}{11}$ and $\dfrac{19}{17}$

1 and $\dfrac{21}{16}$ $\qquad$ $\dfrac{24}{23}$ and $\dfrac{6}{3}$ $\qquad$ $\dfrac{1}{18}$ and $\dfrac{14}{17}$

$\dfrac{22}{5}$ and $\dfrac{18}{7}$ $\qquad$ $\dfrac{3}{16}$ and $\dfrac{3}{8}$ $\qquad$ $\dfrac{24}{23}$ and $1\dfrac{9}{10}$

$\frac{6}{15}$ and $\frac{1}{22}$ $\frac{23}{19}$ and $\frac{10}{6}$ $\frac{15}{12}$ and 1

$1\frac{19}{20}$ and $\frac{20}{14}$ $\frac{4}{7}$ and $\frac{7}{8}$ $\frac{18}{16}$ and $\frac{10}{7}$

3 and $\frac{13}{4}$ $\frac{24}{23}$ and $\frac{5}{4}$ $\frac{1}{20}$ and $\frac{8}{17}$

$\frac{23}{8}$ and $\frac{24}{22}$ $\frac{2}{8}$ and $\frac{8}{9}$ $\frac{23}{13}$ and $1\frac{19}{20}$

$\frac{5}{8}$ and $\frac{7}{11}$ $\frac{24}{23}$ and $\frac{23}{17}$ $\frac{17}{15}$ and 2

1 $\dfrac{2}{14}$ and $\dfrac{19}{18}$ $\dfrac{1}{23}$ and $\dfrac{7}{9}$ $\dfrac{17}{7}$ and $\dfrac{22}{16}$

1   and $\dfrac{22}{20}$ $\dfrac{24}{19}$ and $\dfrac{21}{9}$ $\dfrac{3}{17}$ and $\dfrac{14}{18}$

$\dfrac{23}{19}$ and $\dfrac{13}{5}$ $\dfrac{14}{15}$ and $\dfrac{6}{20}$ $\dfrac{22}{16}$ and $1\dfrac{4}{5}$

$\dfrac{1}{4}$ and $\dfrac{1}{3}$ $\dfrac{23}{12}$ and $\dfrac{15}{10}$ $\dfrac{21}{7}$ and 3

2 $\dfrac{2}{4}$ and $\dfrac{16}{7}$ $\dfrac{22}{23}$ and $\dfrac{9}{18}$ $\dfrac{20}{14}$ and $\dfrac{10}{7}$

2 $\quad$ and $\dfrac{24}{13}$ $\qquad$ $\dfrac{14}{10}$ and $\dfrac{24}{21}$ $\qquad$ $\dfrac{4}{6}$ and $\dfrac{1}{4}$

$\dfrac{17}{13}$ and $\dfrac{23}{18}$ $\qquad$ $\dfrac{4}{14}$ and $\dfrac{1}{9}$ $\qquad$ $\dfrac{22}{21}$ and $1\dfrac{21}{23}$

$\dfrac{5}{9}$ and $\dfrac{7}{12}$ $\qquad$ $\dfrac{24}{23}$ and $\dfrac{7}{2}$ $\qquad$ $\dfrac{16}{3}$ and 5

$1\dfrac{1}{2}$ and $\dfrac{24}{19}$ $\qquad$ $\dfrac{2}{4}$ and $\dfrac{11}{14}$ $\qquad$ $\dfrac{17}{10}$ and $\dfrac{18}{9}$

11 $\quad$ and $\dfrac{23}{2}$ $\qquad$ $\dfrac{24}{23}$ and $\dfrac{20}{9}$ $\qquad$ $\dfrac{5}{6}$ and $\dfrac{3}{13}$

$\dfrac{23}{6}$ and $\dfrac{12}{9}$ $\qquad$ $\dfrac{7}{8}$ and $\dfrac{4}{5}$ $\qquad$ $\dfrac{7}{3}$ and $2\dfrac{7}{11}$

$\dfrac{10}{20}$ and $\dfrac{1}{2}$ $\qquad$ $\dfrac{21}{11}$ and $\dfrac{20}{10}$ $\qquad$ $\dfrac{11}{6}$ and 1

$1\dfrac{4}{13}$ and $\dfrac{24}{22}$ $\qquad$ $\dfrac{5}{8}$ and $\dfrac{1}{6}$ $\qquad$ $\dfrac{17}{11}$ and $\dfrac{24}{23}$

2 and $\dfrac{20}{12}$ $\qquad$ $\dfrac{20}{4}$ and $\dfrac{15}{13}$ $\qquad$ $\dfrac{2}{7}$ and $\dfrac{11}{17}$

$\dfrac{9}{6}$ and $\dfrac{24}{5}$ $\qquad$ $\dfrac{2}{15}$ and $\dfrac{3}{15}$ $\qquad$ $\dfrac{18}{14}$ and $1\dfrac{5}{22}$

$\frac{3}{9}$ and $\frac{4}{13}$ $\frac{24}{22}$ and $\frac{10}{7}$ $\frac{17}{6}$ and 2

$1\frac{5}{16}$ and $\frac{23}{20}$ $\frac{2}{21}$ and $\frac{19}{21}$ $\frac{22}{19}$ and $\frac{15}{10}$

2 and $\frac{16}{11}$ $\frac{7}{6}$ and $\frac{18}{12}$ $\frac{21}{23}$ and $\frac{1}{3}$

$\frac{21}{10}$ and $\frac{24}{20}$ $\frac{19}{22}$ and $\frac{1}{6}$ $\frac{20}{19}$ and $1\frac{8}{21}$

$\frac{3}{15}$ and $\frac{2}{6}$ $\frac{10}{2}$ and $\frac{22}{6}$ $\frac{18}{17}$ and 1

1 $\frac{11}{13}$ and $\frac{24}{23}$ $\frac{8}{18}$ and $\frac{2}{5}$ $\frac{21}{9}$ and $\frac{24}{22}$

1   and $\frac{21}{19}$ $\frac{21}{14}$ and $\frac{23}{22}$ $\frac{8}{22}$ and $\frac{3}{7}$

$\frac{10}{5}$ and $\frac{16}{14}$ $\frac{3}{6}$ and $\frac{21}{23}$ $\frac{22}{12}$ and 1 $\frac{5}{22}$

$\frac{8}{11}$ and $\frac{2}{4}$ $\frac{20}{14}$ and $\frac{16}{15}$ $\frac{15}{11}$ and 2

1 $\frac{8}{13}$ and $\frac{18}{13}$ $\frac{16}{18}$ and $\frac{2}{8}$ $\frac{14}{3}$ and $\frac{24}{20}$

1 and $\dfrac{24}{22}$ $\dfrac{13}{12}$ and $\dfrac{24}{15}$ $\dfrac{1}{12}$ and $\dfrac{3}{15}$

$\dfrac{24}{15}$ and $\dfrac{19}{9}$ $\dfrac{2}{17}$ and $\dfrac{3}{13}$ $\dfrac{17}{4}$ and $4\dfrac{3}{23}$

$\dfrac{17}{23}$ and $\dfrac{8}{11}$ $\dfrac{22}{21}$ and $\dfrac{24}{16}$ $\dfrac{23}{17}$ and 2

$1\dfrac{1}{4}$ and $\dfrac{21}{18}$ $\dfrac{6}{11}$ and $\dfrac{7}{20}$ $\dfrac{18}{14}$ and $\dfrac{24}{17}$

1 and $\dfrac{21}{20}$ $\dfrac{22}{19}$ and $\dfrac{11}{4}$ $\dfrac{6}{22}$ and $\dfrac{10}{12}$

8 Adding Fractions

Basic Concepts: Two proper or improper fractions can be added together by first expressing each fraction with the lowest common denominator. Recall that the lowest common denominator was described in Chapter 6, and the technique of expressing two fractions with their lowest common denominator was described in Chapter 7. Once both fractions are expressed with a common denominator, you can add the numerators together. For $\frac{5}{6} + \frac{7}{4}$, we get $\frac{5\times2}{6\times2} + \frac{7\times3}{4\times3} = \frac{10+21}{12} = \frac{31}{12}$.

A fraction can be added to an integer by first writing the integer as a fraction by dividing it by 1. For example, $\frac{3}{4} + 2 = \frac{3}{4} + \frac{2}{1} = \frac{3}{4} + \frac{2\times4}{1\times4} = \frac{3}{4} + \frac{8}{4} = \frac{3+8}{4} = \frac{11}{4}$. Two mixed numbers can be added together by first converting each mixed number into an improper fraction, as described in Chapter 3.

Directions: Add the two given fractions by expressing each fraction with the lowest common denominator, as described above. Reduce your answer when possible (as described in Chapter 5). Express your answer as a mixed number. Study the examples below before you begin. Check your answers in the back of the book.

Examples.

$$\frac{5}{6} + \frac{7}{4} = \frac{5\times2}{6\times2} + \frac{7\times3}{4\times3} = \frac{10+21}{12} = \frac{31}{12} = 2\frac{7}{12}$$

$$\frac{3}{4} + \frac{5}{2} = \frac{3\times1}{4\times1} + \frac{5\times2}{2\times2} = \frac{3+10}{4} = \frac{13}{4} = 3\frac{1}{4}$$

$$\frac{7}{3} + \frac{4}{9} = \frac{7\times3}{3\times3} + \frac{4\times1}{9\times1} = \frac{21+4}{9} = \frac{25}{9} = 2\frac{7}{9}$$

$$3 + \frac{7}{2} = \frac{3}{1} + \frac{7}{2} = \frac{3\times2}{1\times2} + \frac{7\times1}{2\times1} = \frac{6+7}{2} = \frac{13}{2} = 6\frac{1}{2}$$

$$2\frac{3}{4} + 1 = \frac{4\times2+3}{4} + \frac{1}{1} = \frac{11\times1}{4\times1} + \frac{1\times4}{1\times4} = \frac{11+4}{4} = \frac{15}{4} = 3\frac{3}{4}$$

$$1\frac{2}{3} + 5\frac{1}{4} = \frac{3\times1+2}{3} + \frac{4\times5+1}{4} = \frac{5}{3} + \frac{21}{4} = \frac{5\times4}{3\times4} + \frac{21\times3}{4\times3} = \frac{20+63}{12} = \frac{83}{12} = 6\frac{11}{12}$$

$$3\frac{1}{2} + 5\frac{4}{7} = \frac{2\times3+1}{2} + \frac{7\times5+4}{7} = \frac{7}{2} + \frac{39}{7} = \frac{7\times7}{2\times7} + \frac{39\times2}{7\times2} = \frac{49+78}{14} = \frac{127}{14} = 9\frac{1}{14}$$

Note: When adding an integer to a mixed number, as in $2\frac{3}{4} + 1$, you could just add the integers to get $3\frac{3}{4}$ more efficiently.

$\frac{1}{6} + \frac{4}{3}$

$5\frac{2}{5} + 9\frac{1}{3}$

$\frac{8}{9} + 4$

$4\frac{1}{2} + 6\frac{4}{5}$

$\frac{8}{3} + \frac{7}{6}$

$8\frac{3}{5} + 4\frac{4}{9}$

$\frac{7}{9} + \frac{3}{2}$

$8\frac{3}{8} + 1\frac{2}{5}$

$5 + \frac{1}{7}$

$\dfrac{9}{4} + \dfrac{5}{6}$

$3\dfrac{3}{8} + 4\dfrac{1}{3}$

$\dfrac{1}{4} + 5$

$7\dfrac{2}{5} + 1\dfrac{1}{6}$

$\dfrac{5}{2} + \dfrac{1}{8}$

$5\dfrac{2}{9} + 9\dfrac{8}{9}$

$\dfrac{3}{2} + \dfrac{4}{7}$

$9\dfrac{8}{9} + 6\dfrac{5}{9}$

$5 + \dfrac{5}{6}$

$\frac{4}{3} + \frac{4}{3}$

$1\frac{1}{2} + 7\frac{1}{6}$

$\frac{7}{4} + 5$

$4\frac{3}{8} + 8\frac{7}{9}$

$\frac{1}{5} + \frac{5}{8}$

$6\frac{4}{7} + 3\frac{3}{8}$

$\frac{11}{6} + \frac{5}{4}$

$4\frac{5}{6} + 7\frac{7}{9}$

$4 + \frac{7}{2}$

$\dfrac{2}{5} + \dfrac{5}{2}$

$5\dfrac{1}{3} + 5\dfrac{1}{2}$

$\dfrac{3}{7} + 8$

$5\dfrac{1}{2} + 3\dfrac{3}{5}$

$\dfrac{8}{5} + \dfrac{7}{6}$

$1\dfrac{2}{7} + 6\dfrac{5}{6}$

$\dfrac{2}{9} + \dfrac{5}{7}$

$5\dfrac{1}{4} + 9\dfrac{4}{5}$

$4 + \dfrac{3}{2}$

$\frac{11}{7} + \frac{6}{5}$

$4\frac{4}{7} + 4\frac{2}{7}$

$\frac{7}{9} + 8$

$8\frac{4}{9} + 6\frac{3}{5}$

$\frac{5}{2} + \frac{3}{4}$

$3\frac{2}{9} + 6\frac{1}{2}$

$\frac{2}{5} + \frac{1}{9}$

$3\frac{2}{3} + 3\frac{1}{7}$

$9 + \frac{11}{6}$

$$\frac{3}{8} + \frac{9}{5}$$

$$4\frac{4}{9} + 6\frac{5}{6}$$

$$\frac{4}{5} + 3$$

$$3\frac{1}{6} + 3\frac{5}{6}$$

$$\frac{7}{4} + \frac{3}{8}$$

$$2\frac{3}{5} + 8\frac{2}{5}$$

$$\frac{5}{3} + \frac{11}{7}$$

$$1\frac{1}{5} + 1\frac{1}{4}$$

$$5 + \frac{9}{8}$$

$\frac{5}{3} + \frac{6}{5}$

$7\frac{1}{3} + 6\frac{1}{7}$

$\frac{7}{6} + 8$

$5\frac{5}{6} + 4\frac{1}{4}$

$\frac{5}{4} + \frac{5}{6}$

$7\frac{5}{8} + 7\frac{3}{7}$

$\frac{5}{6} + \frac{1}{3}$

$3\frac{2}{7} + 7\frac{3}{4}$

$1 + \frac{7}{2}$

$\frac{2}{7} + \frac{5}{2}$

$7\frac{2}{7} + 3\frac{5}{8}$

$\frac{1}{6} + 8$

$6\frac{1}{7} + 7\frac{1}{2}$

$\frac{1}{5} + \frac{3}{7}$

$5\frac{3}{4} + 2\frac{3}{8}$

$\frac{4}{3} + \frac{4}{3}$

$7\frac{1}{6} + 4\frac{1}{6}$

$5 + \frac{6}{7}$

$\frac{8}{9} + \frac{7}{3}$

$9\frac{1}{4} + 5\frac{5}{7}$

$\frac{3}{8} + 3$

$6\frac{1}{5} + 5\frac{4}{5}$

$\frac{1}{6} + \frac{9}{7}$

$2\frac{3}{7} + 1\frac{1}{2}$

$\frac{7}{2} + \frac{7}{5}$

$8\frac{1}{8} + 7\frac{7}{8}$

$9 + \frac{7}{2}$

$\frac{7}{9} + \frac{3}{4}$

$3\frac{1}{2} + 5\frac{5}{9}$

$\frac{2}{3} + 6$

$7\frac{1}{2} + 6\frac{5}{7}$

$\frac{1}{9} + \frac{7}{5}$

$9\frac{3}{4} + 7\frac{4}{7}$

$\frac{9}{2} + \frac{7}{5}$

$4\frac{1}{2} + 2\frac{4}{5}$

$5 + \frac{3}{5}$

$\frac{1}{6} + \frac{9}{8}$

$7\frac{1}{4} + 5\frac{2}{7}$

$\frac{1}{6} + 8$

$7\frac{3}{5} + 6\frac{4}{5}$

$\frac{5}{3} + \frac{1}{3}$

$2\frac{6}{7} + 5\frac{1}{4}$

$\frac{5}{4} + \frac{7}{8}$

$6\frac{8}{9} + 6\frac{8}{9}$

$8 + \frac{9}{4}$

9 Subtracting Fractions

Basic Concepts: Subtract two proper/improper fractions with the same method that we used for adding them, except for subtracting the numerators after finding the common denominator. See Chapter 8. For example, for $\frac{7}{4} - \frac{5}{6}$, we get $\frac{7\times3}{4\times3} + \frac{5\times2}{6\times2} = \frac{21-10}{12} = \frac{11}{12}$. If the subtraction involves integers or mixed numbers, first express the integers or mixed numbers as improper fractions, as described in Chapter 8.

Directions: Subtract the two given fractions by expressing each fraction with the lowest common denominator, as described above (using the technique from Chapter 8). Reduce your answer when possible (as described in Chapter 5). Express your answer as a mixed number. Study the examples below before you begin. Check your answers in the back of the book.

Examples.

$$\frac{2}{3} - \frac{1}{4} = \frac{2\times4}{3\times4} - \frac{1\times3}{4\times3} = \frac{8-3}{12} = \frac{5}{12}$$

$$\frac{5}{2} - \frac{3}{4} = \frac{5\times4}{2\times4} - \frac{3\times2}{4\times2} = \frac{20-6}{8} = \frac{14}{8} = \frac{14\div2}{8\div2} = \frac{7}{4} = 1\frac{3}{4}$$

$$\frac{7}{3} - \frac{4}{9} = \frac{7\times3}{3\times3} - \frac{4\times1}{9\times1} = \frac{21-4}{9} = \frac{17}{9} = 1\frac{8}{9}$$

$$5 - \frac{7}{2} = \frac{5}{1} - \frac{7}{2} = \frac{5\times2}{1\times2} - \frac{7\times1}{2\times1} = \frac{10-7}{2} = \frac{3}{2} = 1\frac{1}{2}$$

$$2\frac{3}{4} - 1 = \frac{4\times2+3}{4} - \frac{1}{1} = \frac{11\times1}{4\times1} - \frac{1\times4}{1\times4} = \frac{11-4}{4} = \frac{7}{4} = 1\frac{3}{4}$$

$$5\frac{1}{4} - 1\frac{2}{3} = \frac{4\times5+1}{4} - \frac{3\times1+2}{3} = \frac{21}{4} - \frac{5}{3} = \frac{21\times3}{4\times3} - \frac{5\times4}{3\times4} = \frac{63-20}{12} = \frac{43}{12} = 3\frac{7}{12}$$

$$5\frac{4}{7} - 3\frac{1}{2} = \frac{7\times5+4}{7} - \frac{2\times3+1}{2} = \frac{39}{7} - \frac{7}{2} = \frac{39\times2}{7\times2} - \frac{7\times7}{2\times7} = \frac{78-49}{14} = \frac{29}{14} = 2\frac{1}{14}$$

Note: When the subtraction involves a mixed number minus an integer, as in $2\frac{3}{4} - 1$, you could just subtract the integers to get $1\frac{3}{4}$ more efficiently; but it's not quite as simple for an integer minus a mixed number, as in $5 - 3\frac{1}{2}$ (which is $1\frac{1}{2}$, not $2\frac{1}{2}$).

$\frac{9}{8} - \frac{7}{8}$

$3\frac{1}{2} - 1\frac{5}{9}$

$\frac{7}{6} - 1$

$6\frac{4}{9} - 4\frac{7}{8}$

$\frac{7}{3} - \frac{1}{4}$

$8\frac{3}{5} - 5\frac{5}{8}$

$\frac{5}{7} - \frac{2}{9}$

$6\frac{7}{9} - 2\frac{2}{3}$

$9 - \frac{1}{9}$

$$\frac{2}{3} - \frac{2}{7} \qquad\qquad 7\frac{4}{5} - 2\frac{1}{7} \qquad\qquad \frac{8}{7} - 1$$

$$6\frac{1}{9} - 4\frac{4}{7} \qquad\qquad \frac{4}{3} - \frac{1}{3} \qquad\qquad 2\frac{1}{3} - 2\frac{1}{4}$$

$$\frac{9}{4} - \frac{2}{9} \qquad\qquad 7\frac{4}{7} - 3\frac{1}{6} \qquad\qquad 5 - \frac{1}{7}$$

$\dfrac{9}{5} - \dfrac{4}{9}$

$8\dfrac{1}{2} - 1\dfrac{8}{9}$

$\dfrac{11}{6} - 1$

$5\dfrac{4}{5} - 1\dfrac{1}{2}$

$\dfrac{9}{8} - \dfrac{1}{3}$

$5\dfrac{1}{2} - 1\dfrac{5}{6}$

$\dfrac{7}{6} - \dfrac{5}{8}$

$7\dfrac{1}{6} - 2\dfrac{1}{2}$

$4 - \dfrac{8}{9}$

$$\frac{8}{5} - \frac{1}{8}$$

$$4\frac{2}{3} - 1\frac{1}{4}$$

$$\frac{11}{6} - 1$$

$$6\frac{1}{2} - 3\frac{3}{4}$$

$$\frac{13}{7} - \frac{1}{2}$$

$$6\frac{6}{7} - 1\frac{1}{4}$$

$$\frac{9}{5} - \frac{7}{8}$$

$$3\frac{1}{4} - 2\frac{1}{9}$$

$$6 - \frac{6}{5}$$

$$\frac{5}{4} - \frac{7}{9} \qquad 6\frac{1}{2} - 3\frac{3}{4} \qquad \frac{8}{3} - 2$$

$$5\frac{4}{7} - 1\frac{1}{2} \qquad \frac{9}{4} - \frac{5}{8} \qquad 7\frac{1}{5} - 4\frac{2}{3}$$

$$\frac{8}{9} - \frac{2}{3} \qquad 2\frac{3}{7} - 1\frac{1}{2} \qquad 5 - \frac{4}{3}$$

$$\frac{8}{3} - \frac{5}{2} \qquad\qquad 2\frac{4}{5} - 1\frac{7}{9} \qquad\qquad \frac{9}{8} - 1$$

$$9\frac{3}{8} - 3\frac{1}{2} \qquad\qquad \frac{9}{5} - \frac{4}{3} \qquad\qquad 9\frac{5}{6} - 1\frac{1}{9}$$

$$\frac{7}{4} - \frac{5}{3} \qquad\qquad 8\frac{1}{3} - 4\frac{1}{3} \qquad\qquad 7 - \frac{6}{7}$$

$\frac{2}{9} - \frac{1}{9}$

$9\frac{1}{2} - 5\frac{1}{5}$

$\frac{10}{9} - 1$

$4\frac{1}{2} - 1\frac{1}{7}$

$\frac{7}{9} - \frac{1}{9}$

$6\frac{4}{7} - 2\frac{2}{3}$

$\frac{5}{9} - \frac{2}{5}$

$9\frac{6}{7} - 2\frac{1}{6}$

$11 - \frac{9}{4}$

$$\frac{6}{5} - \frac{9}{8}$$

$$9\frac{8}{9} - 9\frac{1}{6}$$

$$\frac{7}{2} - 1$$

$$9\frac{1}{7} - 1\frac{1}{2}$$

$$\frac{11}{7} - \frac{7}{6}$$

$$5\frac{3}{5} - 5\frac{1}{2}$$

$$\frac{5}{6} - \frac{1}{3}$$

$$8\frac{1}{9} - 4\frac{3}{8}$$

$$7 - \frac{13}{7}$$

$$\frac{4}{3} - \frac{1}{2} \qquad\qquad 5\frac{5}{8} - 4\frac{1}{2} \qquad\qquad \frac{10}{9} - 1$$

$$3\frac{1}{4} - 1\frac{3}{4} \qquad\qquad \frac{3}{2} - \frac{2}{9} \qquad\qquad 9\frac{5}{6} - 9\frac{3}{4}$$

$$\frac{7}{2} - \frac{7}{9} \qquad\qquad 9\frac{1}{6} - 1\frac{7}{8} \qquad\qquad 3 - \frac{8}{3}$$

$$\frac{9}{5} - \frac{1}{8} \qquad\qquad 4\frac{5}{7} - 4\frac{1}{6} \qquad\qquad \frac{10}{9} - 1$$

$$8\frac{1}{2} - 5\frac{1}{4} \qquad\qquad \frac{5}{9} - \frac{3}{7} \qquad\qquad 3\frac{4}{9} - 1\frac{8}{9}$$

$$\frac{3}{7} - \frac{1}{5} \qquad\qquad 4\frac{2}{3} - 1\frac{6}{7} \qquad\qquad 1 - \frac{1}{4}$$

$$\frac{7}{3} - \frac{\#}{6}$$

$$8\frac{1}{2} - 7\frac{1}{2}$$

$$\frac{7}{6} - 1$$

$$7\frac{3}{5} - 4\frac{2}{7}$$

$$\frac{5}{3} - \frac{3}{2}$$

$$6\frac{5}{6} - 2\frac{5}{6}$$

$$\frac{5}{2} - \frac{3}{5}$$

$$4\frac{7}{9} - 2\frac{5}{6}$$

$$9 - \frac{11}{7}$$

10 Multiplying Fractions

Basic Concepts: Proper or improper fractions, like $\frac{5}{6}$ and $\frac{9}{4}$, can be multiplied together as follows: Multiply the numerators together to form the numerator of the product and multiply the denominators together to form the denominator of the product. For $\frac{5}{6} \times \frac{9}{4}$, we get $\frac{5 \times 9}{6 \times 4} = \frac{45}{24}$, which reduces to $\frac{15}{8}$ by dividing both numerator and denominator by the greatest common factor, which is 3. Note that we could have reduced $\frac{9}{6}$ to $\frac{3}{2}$ before multiplying, writing $\frac{5}{6} \times \frac{9}{4} = \frac{5}{2} \times \frac{3}{4} = \frac{15}{8}$. The solution may be somewhat simpler if you reduce before multiplying.

If the multiplication involves an integer, first express the integer as a fraction by dividing by 1. For example, $\frac{4}{3} \times 2 = \frac{4}{3} \times \frac{2}{1} = \frac{4 \times 2}{3 \times 1} = \frac{8}{3}$. Two mixed numbers can be multiplied together by first converting each mixed number into an improper fraction, as described in Chapter 3.

Directions: Multiply the two given fractions as described above. Reduce your answer when possible (as described in Chapter 5). Express your answer as a mixed number. Study the examples below before you begin. Check your answers in the back of the book.

Examples.

$$\frac{2}{3} \times \frac{1}{4} = \frac{2 \times 1}{3 \times 4} = \frac{2}{12} = \frac{1}{6} \quad \text{or} \quad \frac{2}{3} \times \frac{1}{4} = \frac{1}{3} \times \frac{1}{2} = \frac{1 \times 1}{3 \times 2} = \frac{1}{6}$$

$$\frac{3}{4} \times \frac{5}{9} = \frac{3 \times 5}{4 \times 9} = \frac{15}{36} = \frac{5}{12} \quad \text{or} \quad \frac{3}{4} \times \frac{5}{9} = \frac{1}{4} \times \frac{5}{3} = \frac{1 \times 5}{4 \times 3} = \frac{5}{12}$$

$$\frac{7}{3} \times \frac{4}{9} = \frac{7 \times 4}{3 \times 9} = \frac{28}{27} = 1\frac{1}{27}$$

$$\frac{3}{5} \times 4 = \frac{3}{5} \times \frac{4}{1} = \frac{3 \times 4}{5 \times 1} = \frac{12}{5} = 2\frac{2}{5}$$

$$1\frac{2}{3} \times 5\frac{1}{4} = \frac{3 \times 1 + 2}{3} \times \frac{4 \times 5 + 1}{4} = \frac{5}{3} \times \frac{21}{4} = \frac{5 \times 21}{3 \times 4} = \frac{105}{12} = \frac{105 \div 3}{12 \div 3} = \frac{35}{4} = 8\frac{3}{4}$$

$$3\frac{1}{2} \times 5\frac{4}{7} = \frac{2 \times 3 + 1}{2} \times \frac{7 \times 5 + 4}{7} = \frac{7}{2} \times \frac{39}{7} = \frac{7 \times 39}{2 \times 7} = \frac{273}{14} = \frac{273 \div 7}{14 \div 7} = \frac{39}{2} = 19\frac{1}{2}$$

Note: We could first cancel the 7's in $\frac{7 \times 39}{2 \times 7}$, obtaining $\frac{39}{2}$ more readily.

$\dfrac{5}{2} \times \dfrac{1}{8}$
  $4\dfrac{2}{7} \times 2\dfrac{5}{7}$
  $\dfrac{8}{7} \times 7$

$9\dfrac{1}{4} \times 7\dfrac{1}{6}$
  $\dfrac{10}{7} \times \dfrac{4}{3}$
  $7\dfrac{5}{6} \times 4\dfrac{1}{9}$

$\dfrac{5}{8} \times \dfrac{9}{7}$
  $9\dfrac{1}{6} \times 8\dfrac{1}{7}$
  $2 \times \dfrac{1}{7}$

$$\frac{11}{6} \times \frac{7}{4} \qquad\qquad 9\frac{1}{6} \times 1\frac{4}{9} \qquad\qquad \frac{1}{2} \times 6$$

$$5\frac{1}{4} \times 9\frac{1}{9} \qquad\qquad \frac{1}{2} \times \frac{5}{3} \qquad\qquad 8\frac{1}{8} \times 6\frac{1}{3}$$

$$\frac{3}{2} \times \frac{1}{6} \qquad\qquad 1\frac{2}{3} \times 8\frac{3}{7} \qquad\qquad 6 \times \frac{8}{9}$$

$\frac{1}{8} \times \frac{8}{9}$

$2\frac{2}{5} \times 6\frac{7}{8}$

$\frac{4}{9} \times 8$

$3\frac{1}{3} \times 8\frac{7}{8}$

$\frac{13}{7} \times \frac{1}{8}$

$3\frac{2}{3} \times 5\frac{1}{6}$

$\frac{7}{5} \times \frac{7}{3}$

$7\frac{1}{2} \times 6\frac{1}{3}$

$8 \times \frac{2}{3}$

$$\frac{4}{5} \times \frac{1}{4} \qquad 7\frac{1}{5} \times 6\frac{5}{9} \qquad \frac{5}{4} \times 2$$

$$1\frac{7}{8} \times 7\frac{3}{4} \qquad \frac{3}{2} \times \frac{3}{5} \qquad 7\frac{3}{4} \times 9\frac{3}{5}$$

$$\frac{3}{8} \times \frac{9}{5} \qquad 8\frac{1}{2} \times 3\frac{7}{9} \qquad 8 \times \frac{2}{9}$$

$$\frac{2}{9} \times \frac{8}{3} \qquad 5\frac{5}{9} \times 4\frac{8}{9} \qquad \frac{5}{9} \times 1$$

$$5\frac{3}{8} \times 8\frac{7}{8} \qquad \frac{4}{5} \times \frac{3}{8} \qquad 8\frac{1}{8} \times 2\frac{5}{7}$$

$$\frac{3}{8} \times \frac{4}{9} \qquad 6\frac{3}{5} \times 5\frac{1}{4} \qquad 7 \times \frac{9}{2}$$

$\frac{2}{7} \times \frac{3}{4}$

$2\frac{3}{4} \times 6\frac{2}{5}$

$\frac{7}{3} \times 9$

$5\frac{2}{5} \times 5\frac{3}{4}$

$\frac{8}{5} \times \frac{7}{4}$

$9\frac{2}{9} \times 5\frac{1}{4}$

$\frac{7}{4} \times \frac{1}{4}$

$7\frac{1}{6} \times 1\frac{8}{9}$

$4 \times \frac{5}{9}$

$$\frac{6}{5} \times \frac{8}{3} \qquad\qquad 8\frac{1}{2} \times 6\frac{1}{2} \qquad\qquad \frac{8}{5} \times 2$$

$$8\frac{1}{3} \times 4\frac{5}{6} \qquad\qquad \frac{5}{8} \times \frac{4}{5} \qquad\qquad 2\frac{1}{5} \times 3\frac{2}{5}$$

$$\frac{11}{6} \times \frac{5}{6} \qquad\qquad 7\frac{1}{3} \times 9\frac{2}{3} \qquad\qquad 8 \times \frac{9}{8}$$

$$\frac{7}{9} \times \frac{5}{4}$$

$$3\frac{8}{9} \times 5\frac{1}{7}$$

$$\frac{2}{5} \times 1$$

$$9\frac{3}{4} \times 4\frac{3}{8}$$

$$\frac{3}{5} \times \frac{9}{8}$$

$$1\frac{3}{7} \times 7\frac{5}{8}$$

$$\frac{7}{3} \times \frac{9}{4}$$

$$3\frac{3}{8} \times 9\frac{3}{8}$$

$$9 \times \frac{9}{7}$$

$$\frac{7}{9} \times \frac{7}{6} \qquad 8\frac{1}{2} \times 9\frac{1}{6} \qquad \frac{1}{3} \times 7$$

$$6\frac{6}{7} \times 5\frac{1}{9} \qquad \frac{13}{7} \times \frac{5}{8} \qquad 2\frac{1}{4} \times 2\frac{3}{5}$$

$$\frac{7}{9} \times \frac{7}{9} \qquad 8\frac{8}{9} \times 5\frac{7}{9} \qquad 2 \times \frac{3}{4}$$

$$\frac{3}{8} \times \frac{3}{2} \qquad 7\frac{1}{4} \times 4\frac{1}{3} \qquad \frac{5}{6} \times 9$$

$$7\frac{5}{8} \times 3\frac{2}{3} \qquad \frac{2}{7} \times \frac{9}{2} \qquad 1\frac{3}{5} \times 7\frac{4}{9}$$

$$\frac{7}{4} \times \frac{7}{3} \qquad 9\frac{1}{7} \times 2\frac{1}{8} \qquad 1 \times \frac{2}{3}$$

$$\frac{4}{5} \times \frac{3}{4}$$

$$1\frac{5}{6} \times 9\frac{4}{5}$$

$$\frac{11}{6} \times 7$$

$$1\frac{5}{8} \times 9\frac{2}{3}$$

$$\frac{2}{9} \times \frac{1}{7}$$

$$8\frac{1}{6} \times 7\frac{3}{4}$$

$$\frac{7}{8} \times \frac{5}{3}$$

$$8\frac{2}{7} \times 7\frac{2}{5}$$

$$6 \times \frac{7}{4}$$

11 Reciprocating Fractions, Integers, and Mixed Numbers

Basic Concepts: The reciprocal of a fraction is found by swapping the numerator and denominator. For example, the reciprocal of $\frac{4}{3}$ is $\frac{3}{4}$. Similarly, the reciprocal of $\frac{3}{4}$ is $\frac{4}{3}$.

To find the reciprocal of an integer, first express the integer as an improper fraction by dividing by 1. For example, for the reciprocal of 4, first write $4 = \frac{4}{1}$, from which the reciprocal is found to be $\frac{1}{4}$. Note that the reciprocal of $\frac{1}{4}$ is $\frac{4}{1}$, which reduces to 4.

To find the reciprocal of a mixed number, first convert the mixed number to an improper fraction as described in Chapter 3. For example, for the reciprocal of $1\frac{3}{4}$, first write $1\frac{3}{4} = \frac{4\times1+3}{4} = \frac{7}{4}$, from which the reciprocal is found to be $\frac{4}{7}$.

Directions: Find the reciprocal of each given fraction, integer, or mixed number as described above. Express your answer as a proper or improper fraction, or an integer (but not as a mixed number). Study the examples below before you begin. Check your answers in the back of the book.

Example 1. Find the reciprocal of $\frac{2}{3}$. Swap the numerator and denominator to get $\frac{3}{2}$.

Example 2. Find the reciprocal of $\frac{8}{5}$. Swap the numerator and denominator to get $\frac{5}{8}$.

Example 3. Find the reciprocal of $\frac{1}{6}$. Swap the numerator and denominator to get $\frac{6}{1}$, which reduces to 6.

Example 4. Find the reciprocal of 3. First write $3 = \frac{3}{1}$. Then swap the numerator and denominator to get $\frac{1}{3}$.

Example 5. Find the reciprocal of $2\frac{1}{4}$. First write $2\frac{1}{4} = \frac{4\times2+1}{4} = \frac{9}{4}$. Swap the numerator and denominator to get $\frac{4}{9}$.

$$\frac{7}{4}$$

$$1\frac{4}{7}$$

$$\frac{5}{4}$$

$$3\frac{1}{7}$$

$$\frac{7}{6}$$

$$1\frac{5}{6}$$

$$\frac{2}{3}$$

$$8$$

$$\frac{9}{4}$$

$$7\frac{1}{9}$$

$$\frac{5}{3}$$

$$8\frac{1}{6}$$

$$\frac{7}{9}$$

$$1\frac{1}{3}$$

$$\frac{8}{7}$$

$$\frac{3}{4}$$

$$2\,\frac{5}{9}$$

$$\frac{7}{3}$$

$$5\,\frac{1}{2}$$

$$\frac{3}{2}$$

$$2\,\frac{4}{9}$$

$$\frac{1}{6}$$

$$4$$

$$\frac{1}{8}$$

$$7\,\frac{1}{4}$$

$$\frac{7}{5}$$

$$5\,\frac{1}{3}$$

$$\frac{3}{4}$$

$$4\,\frac{7}{9}$$

$$\frac{1}{3}$$

$\dfrac{11}{6}$

$6\,\dfrac{3}{5}$

$\dfrac{5}{6}$

$5\,\dfrac{7}{8}$

$\dfrac{7}{6}$

$4\,\dfrac{1}{2}$

$\dfrac{9}{2}$

7

$\dfrac{7}{5}$

$5\,\dfrac{1}{6}$

$\dfrac{6}{5}$

$8\,\dfrac{1}{6}$

$\dfrac{2}{9}$

$8\,\dfrac{1}{4}$

$\dfrac{1}{8}$

$\dfrac{9}{2}$

$9\,\dfrac{3}{5}$

$\dfrac{1}{4}$

$4\,\dfrac{7}{8}$

$\dfrac{7}{4}$

$6\,\dfrac{1}{8}$

$\dfrac{2}{3}$

2

$\dfrac{1}{9}$

$6\,\dfrac{3}{4}$

$\dfrac{3}{8}$

$6\,\dfrac{1}{2}$

$\dfrac{7}{2}$

$8\,\dfrac{5}{7}$

$\dfrac{7}{3}$

$\dfrac{1}{4}$

$8\,\dfrac{4}{5}$

$\dfrac{4}{3}$

$6\,\dfrac{5}{9}$

$\dfrac{6}{7}$

$5\,\dfrac{2}{7}$

$\dfrac{1}{6}$

6

$\dfrac{2}{5}$

$1\,\dfrac{3}{4}$

$\dfrac{11}{6}$

$4\,\dfrac{7}{8}$

$\dfrac{3}{5}$

$3\,\dfrac{1}{9}$

$\dfrac{2}{9}$

$\dfrac{1}{3}$

$2\dfrac{3}{7}$

$\dfrac{4}{3}$

$6\dfrac{1}{8}$

$\dfrac{1}{2}$

$2\dfrac{1}{6}$

$\dfrac{9}{2}$

7

$\dfrac{7}{2}$

$3\dfrac{1}{2}$

$\dfrac{7}{6}$

$5\dfrac{3}{8}$

$\dfrac{5}{3}$

$4\dfrac{7}{8}$

$\dfrac{3}{5}$

$$\frac{1}{8}$$

$$2\,\frac{5}{8}$$

$$\frac{3}{2}$$

$$7\,\frac{8}{9}$$

$$\frac{3}{2}$$

$$9\,\frac{1}{8}$$

$$\frac{4}{9}$$

$$9$$

$$\frac{2}{5}$$

$$6\,\frac{1}{6}$$

$$\frac{7}{3}$$

$$1\,\frac{2}{5}$$

$$\frac{4}{5}$$

$$4\,\frac{1}{2}$$

$$\frac{1}{4}$$

$\dfrac{1}{9}$ $3\dfrac{1}{5}$ $\dfrac{9}{8}$

$5\dfrac{1}{6}$ $\dfrac{13}{7}$ $8\dfrac{1}{7}$

$\dfrac{9}{4}$ 4 $\dfrac{11}{7}$

$1\dfrac{3}{8}$ $\dfrac{7}{3}$ $3\dfrac{1}{2}$

$\dfrac{7}{8}$ $8\dfrac{4}{7}$ $\dfrac{8}{5}$

$\dfrac{8}{7}$

$9\,\dfrac{4}{5}$

$\dfrac{8}{9}$

$4\,\dfrac{4}{9}$

$\dfrac{7}{6}$

$8\,\dfrac{3}{7}$

$\dfrac{7}{2}$

8

$\dfrac{8}{3}$

$4\,\dfrac{4}{7}$

$\dfrac{1}{8}$

$6\,\dfrac{2}{3}$

$\dfrac{1}{8}$

$1\,\dfrac{2}{3}$

$\dfrac{1}{4}$

$\dfrac{3}{4}$ $\qquad$ $4\,\dfrac{2}{7}$ $\qquad$ $\dfrac{3}{5}$

$7\,\dfrac{1}{6}$ $\qquad$ $\dfrac{1}{8}$ $\qquad$ $1\,\dfrac{3}{8}$

$\dfrac{5}{6}$ $\qquad$ 9 $\qquad$ $\dfrac{9}{7}$

$8\,\dfrac{3}{4}$ $\qquad$ $\dfrac{7}{2}$ $\qquad$ $4\,\dfrac{1}{9}$

$\dfrac{10}{7}$ $\qquad$ $9\,\dfrac{2}{9}$ $\qquad$ $\dfrac{12}{7}$

$$\frac{13}{7}$$

$$4\frac{1}{2}$$

$$\frac{3}{7}$$

$$1\frac{1}{4}$$

$$\frac{8}{5}$$

$$1\frac{3}{5}$$

$$\frac{5}{3}$$

$$2$$

$$\frac{8}{3}$$

$$1\frac{1}{5}$$

$$\frac{7}{6}$$

$$2\frac{2}{3}$$

$$\frac{1}{5}$$

$$1\frac{1}{2}$$

$$\frac{8}{7}$$

12 Dividing Fractions

Basic Concepts: When one fraction is divided by another, as in $\frac{5}{6} \div \frac{4}{9}$, the first fraction, $\frac{5}{6}$, is called the **dividend**, the second fraction, $\frac{4}{9}$, is called the **divisor**, and the result is called the **quotient**. Note that the divisor comes after the $\div$ sign.

Proper or improper fractions, like $\frac{5}{6}$ and $\frac{9}{4}$, can be divided as follows: First find the reciprocal of the divisor (the fraction that comes after the $\div$ sign), and then multiply the dividend with the reciprocal of the divisor. See Chapter 11 regarding how to find the reciprocal of a fraction and Chapter 10 regarding how to multiply proper or improper fractions together. For $\frac{5}{6} \div \frac{4}{9}$, we multiply $\frac{5}{6}$ by the reciprocal of $\frac{4}{9}$, which is $\frac{9}{4}$, to get $\frac{5}{6} \times \frac{9}{4} = \frac{5 \times 9}{6 \times 4} = \frac{45}{24}$, which reduces to $\frac{15}{8}$.

If one number is an integer, first express the integer as an improper fraction by dividing by 1. For example, $2 \div \frac{1}{4} = \frac{2}{1} \div \frac{1}{4} = \frac{2}{1} \times \frac{4}{1} = \frac{2 \times 4}{1 \times 1} = \frac{8}{1} = 8$. Two mixed numbers can be divided by first converting each mixed number into an improper fraction, as described in Chapter 3.

Directions: Divide the two given fractions as described above. Reduce your answer when possible (as described in Chapter 5). Express your answer as a mixed number. Study the examples below before you begin. Check your answers in the back of the book.

Examples.

$$\frac{2}{3} \div \frac{1}{4} = \frac{2}{3} \times \frac{4}{1} = \frac{2 \times 4}{3 \times 1} = \frac{8}{3} = 2\frac{2}{3}$$

$$\frac{3}{4} \div \frac{9}{5} = \frac{3}{4} \times \frac{5}{9} = \frac{3 \times 5}{4 \times 9} = \frac{15}{36} = \frac{15 \div 3}{36 \div 3} = \frac{5}{12}$$

$$\frac{7}{3} \div \frac{4}{9} = \frac{7}{3} \times \frac{9}{4} = \frac{7 \times 9}{3 \times 4} = \frac{63}{12} = \frac{63 \div 3}{12 \div 3} = \frac{21}{4} = 5\frac{1}{4}$$

$$\frac{3}{2} \div 4 = \frac{3}{2} \div \frac{4}{1} = \frac{3}{2} \times \frac{1}{4} = \frac{3 \times 1}{2 \times 4} = \frac{3}{8}$$

$$2 \div \frac{1}{4} = \frac{2}{1} \div \frac{1}{4} = \frac{2}{1} \times \frac{4}{1} = \frac{2 \times 4}{1 \times 1} = \frac{8}{1} = 8$$

$$1\frac{2}{3} \div 5\frac{1}{4} = \frac{3 \times 1 + 2}{3} \div \frac{4 \times 5 + 1}{4} = \frac{5}{3} \div \frac{21}{4} = \frac{5}{3} \times \frac{4}{21} = \frac{5 \times 4}{3 \times 21} = \frac{20}{63}$$

$$5\frac{4}{7} \div 3\frac{1}{2} = \frac{7 \times 5 + 4}{7} \div \frac{2 \times 3 + 1}{2} = \frac{39}{7} \div \frac{7}{2} = \frac{39}{7} \times \frac{2}{7} = \frac{39 \times 2}{7 \times 7} = \frac{78}{49} = 1\frac{29}{49}$$

$$2\frac{1}{4} \div 1\frac{3}{8} = \frac{4 \times 2 + 1}{4} \div \frac{8 \times 1 + 3}{8} = \frac{9}{4} \div \frac{11}{8} = \frac{9}{4} \times \frac{8}{11} = \frac{9 \times 8}{4 \times 11} = \frac{72}{44} = \frac{72 \div 4}{44 \div 4} = \frac{18}{11} = 1\frac{7}{11}$$

$$\frac{5}{4} \div \frac{5}{4} \qquad\qquad 7\frac{3}{4} \div 3\frac{5}{6} \qquad\qquad \frac{5}{4} \div 6$$

$$4\frac{7}{9} \div 7\frac{2}{3} \qquad\qquad \frac{1}{8} \div \frac{7}{9} \qquad\qquad 5\frac{1}{4} \div 3\frac{7}{9}$$

$$\frac{9}{2} \div \frac{3}{4} \qquad\qquad 2\frac{7}{8} \div 2\frac{3}{8} \qquad\qquad 5 \div \frac{2}{9}$$

$$\frac{1}{3} \div \frac{5}{8} \qquad\qquad 8\frac{2}{3} \div 7\frac{1}{5} \qquad\qquad \frac{11}{6} \div 3$$

$$9\frac{2}{9} \div 6\frac{1}{2} \qquad\qquad \frac{2}{3} \div \frac{1}{6} \qquad\qquad 2\frac{2}{7} \div 8\frac{1}{5}$$

$$\frac{7}{6} \div \frac{7}{8} \qquad\qquad 1\frac{4}{5} \div 5\frac{1}{6} \qquad\qquad 2 \div \frac{2}{9}$$

$$\frac{3}{2} \div \frac{3}{5} \qquad 7\frac{1}{3} \div 9\frac{1}{3} \qquad \frac{4}{7} \div 3$$

$$3\frac{7}{8} \div 3\frac{4}{9} \qquad \frac{5}{6} \div \frac{2}{5} \qquad 6\frac{2}{7} \div 6\frac{7}{9}$$

$$\frac{4}{9} \div \frac{8}{5} \qquad 9\frac{4}{9} \div 3\frac{1}{9} \qquad 6 \div \frac{4}{9}$$

$$\frac{10}{7} \div \frac{11}{6}$$

$$6\frac{1}{8} \div 3\frac{3}{4}$$

$$\frac{5}{9} \div 2$$

$$7\frac{1}{4} \div 2\frac{5}{6}$$

$$\frac{13}{7} \div \frac{1}{4}$$

$$7\frac{5}{7} \div 5\frac{2}{9}$$

$$\frac{11}{6} \div \frac{7}{5}$$

$$3\frac{1}{3} \div 9\frac{5}{6}$$

$$8 \div \frac{5}{3}$$

$\dfrac{12}{7} \div \dfrac{1}{9}$

$7\dfrac{2}{9} \div 9\dfrac{4}{9}$

$\dfrac{3}{4} \div 1$

$8\dfrac{1}{4} \div 5\dfrac{5}{6}$

$\dfrac{5}{8} \div \dfrac{1}{3}$

$8\dfrac{1}{2} \div 6\dfrac{2}{3}$

$\dfrac{11}{6} \div \dfrac{1}{6}$

$2\dfrac{3}{4} \div 8\dfrac{3}{5}$

$6 \div \dfrac{1}{7}$

$$\frac{9}{4} \div \frac{1}{9} \qquad\qquad 8\frac{7}{9} \div 1\frac{1}{2} \qquad\qquad \frac{3}{2} \div 2$$

$$5\frac{1}{3} \div 4\frac{1}{2} \qquad\qquad \frac{4}{5} \div \frac{11}{6} \qquad\qquad 6\frac{7}{9} \div 2\frac{3}{5}$$

$$\frac{9}{8} \div \frac{6}{7} \qquad\qquad 3\frac{3}{4} \div 3\frac{2}{9} \qquad\qquad 1 \div \frac{7}{2}$$

$$\frac{7}{9} \div \frac{9}{4}$$

$$3\frac{4}{9} \div 6\frac{4}{5}$$

$$\frac{1}{6} \div 8$$

$$3\frac{2}{9} \div 6\frac{1}{2}$$

$$\frac{7}{5} \div \frac{5}{2}$$

$$7\frac{1}{2} \div 3\frac{1}{6}$$

$$\frac{1}{2} \div \frac{1}{4}$$

$$9\frac{2}{9} \div 4\frac{1}{7}$$

$$4 \div \frac{7}{6}$$

$$\frac{8}{3} \div \frac{1}{6} \qquad\qquad 2\frac{2}{3} \div 4\frac{1}{4} \qquad\qquad \frac{3}{2} \div 7$$

$$9\frac{1}{3} \div 3\frac{5}{8} \qquad\qquad \frac{8}{7} \div \frac{10}{7} \qquad\qquad 3\frac{7}{8} \div 4\frac{1}{4}$$

$$\frac{7}{2} \div \frac{9}{4} \qquad\qquad 4\frac{1}{4} \div 6\frac{1}{4} \qquad\qquad 6 \div \frac{12}{7}$$

$$\frac{7}{8} \div \frac{3}{4}$$

$$1\frac{5}{6} \div 8\frac{3}{7}$$

$$\frac{5}{2} \div 9$$

$$5\frac{4}{5} \div 5\frac{6}{7}$$

$$\frac{5}{6} \div \frac{3}{4}$$

$$9\frac{1}{4} \div 1\frac{3}{8}$$

$$\frac{9}{4} \div \frac{7}{9}$$

$$3\frac{1}{4} \div 7\frac{4}{9}$$

$$8 \div \frac{4}{9}$$

$$\frac{1}{7} \div \frac{1}{2} \qquad\qquad 4\frac{1}{6} \div 8\frac{3}{4} \qquad\qquad \frac{5}{2} \div 7$$

$$4\frac{4}{9} \div 5\frac{1}{2} \qquad\qquad \frac{8}{3} \div \frac{5}{4} \qquad\qquad 6\frac{1}{2} \div 3\frac{3}{4}$$

$$\frac{11}{6} \div \frac{11}{6} \qquad\qquad 8\frac{3}{4} \div 1\frac{4}{5} \qquad\qquad 6 \div \frac{1}{8}$$

$$\frac{11}{6} \div \frac{5}{8}$$

$$3\frac{1}{4} \div 3\frac{4}{7}$$

$$\frac{12}{7} \div 5$$

$$9\frac{8}{9} \div 5\frac{3}{8}$$

$$\frac{3}{4} \div \frac{6}{5}$$

$$3\frac{2}{9} \div 1\frac{5}{6}$$

$$\frac{11}{6} \div \frac{7}{6}$$

$$6\frac{3}{7} \div 1\frac{1}{2}$$

$$7 \div \frac{1}{8}$$

Answers

Chapter 1

Note: Only the answers to the gray questions are given for Chapter 1. To get the answers to the white questions, keep the same denominator and subtract the numerator from the denominator. Examples: If gray is $\frac{1}{3}$, white is $\frac{3-1}{3} = \frac{2}{3}$; if gray is $\frac{5}{8}$, white is $\frac{8-5}{8} = \frac{3}{8}$; and if gray is $\frac{3}{4}$, white is $\frac{4-3}{4} = \frac{1}{4}$.

Page 6

$\frac{1}{3}$, $\frac{3}{4}$, $\frac{2}{5}$, $\frac{1}{6}$

$\frac{1}{4}$, $\frac{1}{5}$, $\frac{5}{6}$, $\frac{5}{7}$

$\frac{3}{5}$, $\frac{3}{6}$ or $\frac{1}{2}$, $\frac{2}{7}$, $\frac{5}{8}$

Page 7

$\frac{4}{6}$ or $\frac{2}{3}$, $\frac{3}{7}$, $\frac{2}{8}$ or $\frac{1}{4}$, $\frac{8}{9}$

$\frac{2}{6}$ or $\frac{1}{3}$, $\frac{6}{7}$, $\frac{3}{8}$, $\frac{4}{9}$

$\frac{1}{7}$, $\frac{4}{8}$ or $\frac{1}{2}$, $\frac{6}{9}$ or $\frac{2}{3}$, $\frac{7}{10}$

Page 8

$\frac{1}{8}$, $\frac{7}{9}$, $\frac{5}{10}$ or $\frac{1}{2}$, $\frac{11}{12}$

$\frac{6}{8}$ or $\frac{3}{4}$, $\frac{3}{9}$ or $\frac{1}{3}$, $\frac{2}{10}$ or $\frac{1}{5}$, $\frac{5}{12}$

$\frac{7}{8}$, $\frac{5}{9}$, $\frac{8}{10}$ or $\frac{4}{5}$, $\frac{9}{12}$ or $\frac{3}{4}$

Page 9

$\frac{2}{4}$ or $\frac{1}{2}$, $\frac{2}{5}$, $\frac{3}{6}$ or $\frac{1}{2}$, $\frac{5}{7}$

$\frac{3}{5}$, $\frac{4}{6}$ or $\frac{2}{3}$, $\frac{4}{7}$, $\frac{2}{8}$ or $\frac{1}{4}$

$\frac{3}{6}$ or $\frac{1}{2}$, $\frac{3}{7}$, $\frac{4}{8}$ or $\frac{1}{2}$, $\frac{6}{9}$ or $\frac{2}{3}$

Page 10

$\frac{5}{7}$, $\frac{4}{8}$ or $\frac{1}{2}$, $\frac{4}{9}$, $\frac{7}{10}$

$\frac{3}{7}$, $\frac{6}{8}$ or $\frac{3}{4}$, $\frac{5}{9}$, $\frac{5}{10}$ or $\frac{1}{2}$

$\frac{5}{8}$, $\frac{6}{9}$ or $\frac{2}{3}$, $\frac{7}{10}$, $\frac{6}{12}$ or $\frac{1}{2}$

Page 11

$\frac{4}{8}$ or $\frac{1}{2}$, $\frac{5}{9}$, $\frac{4}{10}$ or $\frac{2}{5}$, $\frac{8}{12}$ or $\frac{2}{3}$

$\frac{5}{8}$, $\frac{3}{9}$ or $\frac{1}{3}$, $\frac{4}{10}$ or $\frac{2}{5}$, $\frac{9}{12}$ or $\frac{3}{4}$

$\frac{4}{8}$ or $\frac{1}{2}$, $\frac{7}{9}$, $\frac{3}{10}$, $\frac{10}{12}$ or $\frac{5}{6}$

Page 12

$1\frac{1}{2}$, $2\frac{1}{3}$, $3\frac{1}{4}$, $1\frac{2}{3}$, $2\frac{3}{4}$

Page 13

$2\frac{1}{4}$, $1\frac{3}{4}$, $3\frac{1}{2}$, $1\frac{5}{6}$, $3\frac{2}{5}$

Chapter 2

Page 15

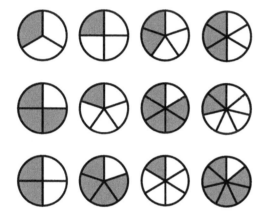

Page 16

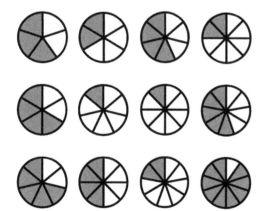

Page 17

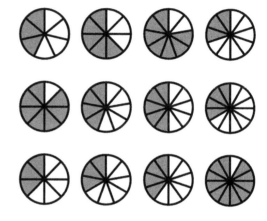

Page 18

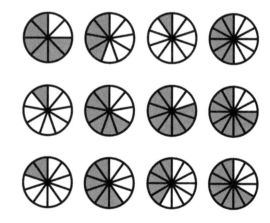

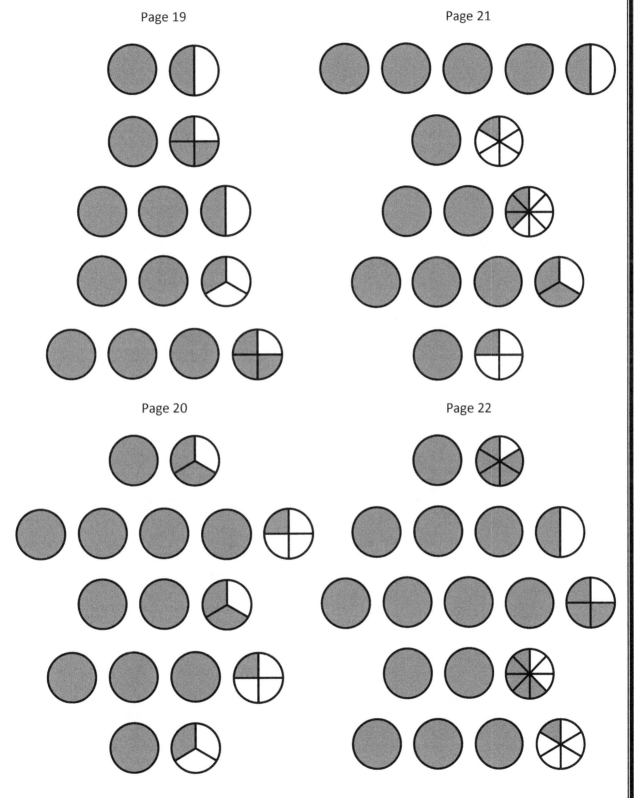

Page 23

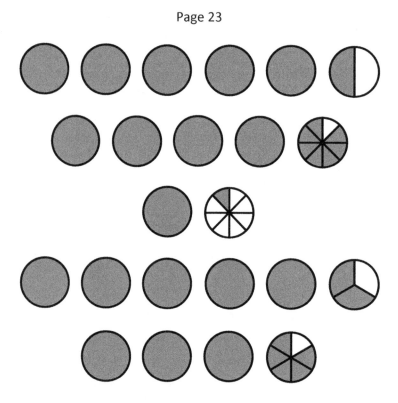

Chapter 3

Page 25

$$\frac{22}{3}, \frac{14}{3}, \frac{31}{4}, \frac{80}{9}$$

$$\frac{59}{8}, \frac{7}{2}, \frac{5}{4}, \frac{47}{9}$$

$$\frac{66}{7}, \frac{37}{5}, \frac{15}{8}, \frac{9}{5}$$

$$\frac{54}{7}, \frac{28}{5}, \frac{57}{8}, \frac{13}{2}$$

$$\frac{9}{2}, \frac{10}{3}, \frac{17}{6}, \frac{56}{9}$$

Page 26

$$\frac{40}{7}, \frac{7}{2}, \frac{17}{5}, \frac{5}{2}$$

$$\frac{25}{9}, \frac{55}{6}, \frac{41}{6}, \frac{13}{2}$$

$$\frac{35}{4}, \frac{19}{2}, \frac{19}{6}, \frac{65}{8}$$

$$\frac{34}{5}, \frac{75}{8}, \frac{35}{8}, \frac{13}{7}$$

$$\frac{67}{8}, \frac{17}{2}, \frac{19}{6}, \frac{17}{6}$$

Page 27

$$\frac{17}{2}, \frac{15}{4}, \frac{17}{5}, \frac{8}{3}$$

$$\frac{11}{4}, \frac{11}{3}, \frac{46}{7}, \frac{41}{9}$$

$$\frac{37}{9}, \frac{13}{2}, \frac{36}{5}, \frac{85}{9}$$

$$\frac{37}{4}, \frac{46}{7}, \frac{8}{3}, \frac{77}{8}$$

$$\frac{3}{2}, \frac{8}{7}, \frac{27}{5}, \frac{29}{9}$$

Page 28

$$\frac{10}{3}, \frac{45}{8}, \frac{26}{3}, \frac{13}{2}$$

$$\frac{8}{3}, \frac{62}{7}, \frac{19}{6}, \frac{61}{9}$$

$$\frac{31}{4}, \frac{19}{8}, \frac{11}{4}, \frac{15}{4}$$

$$\frac{33}{4}, \frac{23}{5}, \frac{66}{7}, \frac{13}{7}$$

$$\frac{17}{2}, \frac{27}{4}, \frac{11}{3}, \frac{47}{6}$$

Page 29

$$\frac{29}{4}, \frac{5}{2}, \frac{20}{3}, \frac{7}{4}$$

$$\frac{15}{8}, \frac{17}{3}, \frac{43}{6}, \frac{39}{5}$$

$$\frac{7}{5}, \frac{14}{3}, \frac{29}{5}, \frac{31}{4}$$

$$\frac{8}{3}, \frac{7}{4}, \frac{45}{7}, \frac{41}{8}$$

$$\frac{22}{7}, \frac{15}{2}, \frac{17}{2}, \frac{89}{9}$$

Page 30

$$\frac{13}{4}, \frac{71}{8}, \frac{19}{8}, \frac{62}{7}$$

$$\frac{3}{2}, \frac{13}{9}, \frac{75}{8}, \frac{9}{8}$$

$$\frac{45}{7}, \frac{47}{8}, \frac{26}{3}, \frac{18}{5}$$

$$\frac{17}{9}, \frac{8}{7}, \frac{29}{6}, \frac{23}{6}$$

$$\frac{15}{4}, \frac{17}{4}, \frac{33}{8}, \frac{23}{4}$$

Page 31

$$\frac{70}{9}, \frac{17}{7}, \frac{39}{5}, \frac{5}{2}$$

$$\frac{11}{2}, \frac{26}{5}, \frac{34}{7}, \frac{23}{3}$$

$$\frac{39}{8}, \frac{55}{8}, \frac{38}{7}, \frac{79}{9}$$

$$\frac{73}{9}, \frac{53}{6}, \frac{36}{5}, \frac{25}{9}$$

$$\frac{74}{9}, \frac{34}{5}, \frac{19}{2}, \frac{44}{7}$$

Page 32

$$\frac{57}{8}, \frac{7}{6}, \frac{73}{9}, \frac{44}{9}$$

$$\frac{31}{7}, \frac{17}{5}, \frac{19}{2}, \frac{13}{8}$$

$$\frac{19}{2}, \frac{7}{3}, \frac{41}{6}, \frac{5}{4}$$

$$\frac{17}{6}, \frac{9}{4}, \frac{15}{8}, \frac{19}{2}$$

$$\frac{3}{2}, \frac{7}{6}, \frac{5}{3}, \frac{5}{4}$$

Page 33

$$\frac{29}{8}, \frac{39}{5}, \frac{16}{9}, \frac{43}{6}$$

$$\frac{16}{7}, \frac{31}{6}, \frac{17}{2}, \frac{26}{3}$$

$$\frac{19}{4}, \frac{43}{6}, \frac{26}{9}, \frac{54}{7}$$

$$\frac{9}{2}, \frac{74}{9}, \frac{25}{9}, \frac{9}{8}$$

$$\frac{17}{8}, \frac{79}{9}, \frac{7}{2}, \frac{61}{9}$$

Page 34

$$\frac{29}{3}, \frac{17}{9}, \frac{45}{8}, \frac{17}{3}$$

$$\frac{19}{2}, \frac{26}{5}, \frac{5}{2}, \frac{19}{2}$$

$$\frac{29}{7}, \frac{37}{6}, \frac{15}{2}, \frac{28}{5}$$

$$\frac{26}{9}, \frac{49}{8}, \frac{31}{4}, \frac{52}{9}$$

$$\frac{20}{3}, \frac{17}{6}, \frac{68}{7}, \frac{3}{2}$$

Page 35

$$\frac{58}{7}, \frac{13}{4}, \frac{13}{3}, \frac{10}{3}$$

$$\frac{57}{8}, \frac{22}{9}, \frac{68}{9}, \frac{11}{3}$$

$$\frac{69}{8}, \frac{9}{5}, \frac{41}{5}, \frac{34}{5}$$

$$\frac{22}{5}, \frac{61}{8}, \frac{30}{7}, \frac{27}{4}$$

$$\frac{16}{3}, \frac{23}{6}, \frac{41}{8}, \frac{11}{4}$$

Chapter 4

Page 37

$4\frac{2}{3}$, $8\frac{3}{4}$, $9\frac{1}{8}$, $4\frac{5}{6}$

$3\frac{5}{6}$, $3\frac{1}{9}$, $8\frac{5}{9}$, $1\frac{5}{6}$

$3\frac{3}{4}$, $5\frac{5}{6}$, $5\frac{7}{9}$, $8\frac{5}{6}$

$1\frac{7}{9}$, $2\frac{2}{5}$, $8\frac{3}{8}$, $9\frac{7}{8}$

$2\frac{2}{3}$, $1\frac{2}{3}$, $8\frac{1}{5}$, $5\frac{1}{2}$

Page 38

$6\frac{5}{6}$, $5\frac{2}{9}$, $1\frac{4}{7}$, $3\frac{1}{7}$

$4\frac{7}{9}$, $1\frac{1}{2}$, $7\frac{1}{8}$, $7\frac{5}{6}$

$4\frac{1}{6}$, $3\frac{5}{9}$, $5\frac{2}{9}$, $5\frac{2}{3}$

$1\frac{1}{7}$, $1\frac{1}{6}$, $6\frac{1}{7}$, $3\frac{1}{3}$

$9\frac{1}{9}$, $7\frac{2}{7}$, $6\frac{2}{5}$, $2\frac{2}{5}$

Page 39

$7\frac{1}{8}$, $7\frac{1}{5}$, $9\frac{3}{7}$, $3\frac{1}{6}$

$7\frac{1}{6}$, $8\frac{1}{4}$, $2\frac{2}{3}$, $5\frac{2}{3}$

$6\frac{8}{9}$, $7\frac{3}{8}$, $6\frac{1}{8}$, $3\frac{3}{4}$

$9\frac{3}{5}$, $2\frac{5}{6}$, $1\frac{2}{3}$, $4\frac{7}{9}$

$2\frac{5}{9}$, $7\frac{2}{3}$, $3\frac{3}{4}$, $5\frac{4}{7}$

Page 40

$2\frac{7}{8}$, $7\frac{5}{9}$, $4\frac{1}{2}$, $3\frac{3}{7}$

$1\frac{5}{6}$, $9\frac{1}{8}$, $3\frac{5}{8}$, $7\frac{7}{8}$

$3\frac{1}{5}$, $6\frac{1}{2}$, $4\frac{2}{5}$, $7\frac{1}{4}$

$7\frac{1}{4}$, $6\frac{4}{5}$, $4\frac{1}{3}$, $5\frac{1}{2}$

$4\frac{6}{7}$, $4\frac{1}{5}$, $4\frac{5}{8}$, $5\frac{8}{9}$

Page 41

$7\frac{1}{2}$, $5\frac{1}{2}$, $9\frac{3}{8}$, $4\frac{4}{5}$

$4\frac{1}{4}$, $5\frac{1}{3}$, $7\frac{5}{6}$, $9\frac{1}{8}$

$2\frac{4}{9}$, $9\frac{1}{4}$, $5\frac{1}{3}$, $2\frac{4}{9}$

$9\frac{1}{2}$, $8\frac{2}{9}$, $6\frac{1}{6}$, $2\frac{1}{9}$

$6\frac{1}{4}$, $8\frac{3}{4}$, $3\frac{2}{7}$, $3\frac{7}{8}$

Page 42

$2\frac{2}{3}$, $6\frac{5}{9}$, $8\frac{1}{7}$, $8\frac{5}{6}$

$9\frac{2}{9}$, $8\frac{1}{2}$, $6\frac{2}{3}$, $4\frac{1}{2}$

$1\frac{1}{7}$, $4\frac{1}{7}$, $9\frac{1}{2}$, $2\frac{1}{6}$

$3\frac{6}{7}$, $8\frac{2}{3}$, $2\frac{5}{6}$, $9\frac{6}{7}$

$9\frac{1}{8}$, $9\frac{1}{3}$, $4\frac{5}{6}$, $6\frac{1}{2}$

Page 43

$2\frac{4}{9}$, $1\frac{4}{7}$, $9\frac{1}{9}$, $9\frac{2}{3}$

$7\frac{3}{5}$, $2\frac{1}{4}$, $1\frac{8}{9}$, $5\frac{4}{7}$

$7\frac{1}{3}$, $8\frac{1}{3}$, $6\frac{3}{8}$, $2\frac{1}{4}$

$3\frac{1}{2}$, $7\frac{2}{3}$, $4\frac{1}{4}$, $9\frac{1}{6}$

$5\frac{5}{7}$, $6\frac{1}{2}$, $9\frac{1}{2}$, $9\frac{1}{7}$

Page 44

$9\frac{1}{2}$, $6\frac{1}{2}$, $8\frac{1}{3}$, $9\frac{2}{5}$

$3\frac{4}{7}$, $7\frac{5}{7}$, $6\frac{1}{4}$, $5\frac{3}{7}$

$8\frac{7}{8}$, $1\frac{5}{6}$, $1\frac{3}{8}$, $5\frac{2}{5}$

$7\frac{1}{3}$, $3\frac{3}{5}$, $2\frac{5}{6}$, $8\frac{1}{3}$

$5\frac{1}{6}$, $6\frac{1}{9}$, $2\frac{2}{3}$, $1\frac{5}{6}$

Page 45

$6\frac{4}{9}$, $4\frac{7}{8}$, $2\frac{3}{4}$, $3\frac{2}{3}$

$7\frac{1}{8}$, $4\frac{2}{5}$, $9\frac{4}{5}$, $6\frac{1}{2}$

$1\frac{1}{2}$, $5\frac{5}{7}$, $2\frac{5}{7}$, $4\frac{3}{8}$

$9\frac{8}{9}$, $2\frac{3}{5}$, $9\frac{1}{2}$, $8\frac{1}{2}$

$7\frac{1}{2}$, $7\frac{2}{9}$, $5\frac{2}{5}$, $2\frac{1}{9}$

Page 46

$6\frac{5}{6}$, $8\frac{2}{3}$, $5\frac{3}{8}$, $8\frac{3}{5}$

$7\frac{3}{8}$, $3\frac{1}{4}$, $7\frac{1}{3}$, $5\frac{1}{2}$

$3\frac{5}{6}$, $7\frac{2}{3}$, $3\frac{3}{8}$, $4\frac{5}{6}$

$5\frac{1}{9}$, $2\frac{8}{9}$, $1\frac{5}{9}$, $2\frac{4}{9}$

$7\frac{1}{2}$, $6\frac{3}{4}$, $9\frac{3}{7}$, $7\frac{4}{7}$

Page 47

$8\frac{5}{6}$, $9\frac{4}{5}$, $9\frac{7}{9}$, $3\frac{1}{3}$

$7\frac{1}{5}$, $5\frac{1}{6}$, $2\frac{2}{9}$, $7\frac{4}{9}$

$1\frac{2}{3}$, $2\frac{5}{7}$, $9\frac{1}{6}$, $6\frac{1}{4}$

$5\frac{1}{6}$, $4\frac{1}{4}$, $9\frac{5}{8}$, $5\frac{3}{4}$

$6\frac{5}{6}$, $8\frac{5}{6}$, $6\frac{2}{3}$, $1\frac{1}{5}$

Chapter 5

Page 49

$\frac{1}{3}$, $9\frac{3}{5}$, $\frac{3}{4}$, $3\frac{3}{4}$

$7\frac{3}{8}$, $\frac{2}{3}$, $7\frac{2}{5}$, $\frac{9}{2}$

$\frac{2}{5}$, $7\frac{7}{9}$, $\frac{3}{8}$, $6\frac{3}{4}$

$9\frac{1}{3}$, $\frac{5}{3}$, $6\frac{6}{7}$, $\frac{1}{5}$

$\frac{8}{9}$, $3\frac{1}{9}$, $\frac{3}{5}$, $2\frac{7}{9}$

Page 50

$1\frac{7}{9}$, $\frac{7}{9}$, $9\frac{4}{7}$, $\frac{5}{4}$

$\frac{9}{5}$, $1\frac{1}{2}$, $\frac{1}{9}$, $9\frac{1}{2}$

$4\frac{4}{5}$, $\frac{9}{8}$, $2\frac{5}{6}$, $\frac{1}{3}$

$\frac{1}{5}$, $6\frac{2}{5}$, $\frac{7}{2}$, $7\frac{2}{3}$

$4\frac{2}{3}$, $\frac{4}{7}$, $5\frac{5}{8}$, $\frac{3}{5}$

Page 51

$\frac{1}{9}$, $8\frac{5}{8}$, $\frac{3}{4}$, $3\frac{3}{4}$

$9\frac{5}{8}$, $\frac{3}{7}$, $9\frac{5}{6}$, $\frac{2}{7}$

$\frac{1}{2}$, $1\frac{2}{5}$, $\frac{1}{8}$, $5\frac{1}{4}$

$5\frac{2}{3}$, $\frac{3}{8}$, $2\frac{2}{5}$, $\frac{3}{8}$

$\frac{2}{3}$, $4\frac{1}{7}$, $\frac{5}{4}$, $5\frac{5}{9}$

Page 52

$8\frac{1}{4}$, $\frac{1}{6}$, $7\frac{3}{4}$, $\frac{3}{4}$

$\frac{8}{5}$, $4\frac{1}{3}$, $\frac{7}{9}$, $2\frac{1}{3}$

$6\frac{1}{6}$, $\frac{5}{4}$, $1\frac{1}{2}$, $\frac{2}{9}$

$\frac{3}{2}$, $7\frac{1}{4}$, $\frac{9}{8}$, $4\frac{5}{8}$

$5\frac{5}{6}$, $\frac{3}{2}$, $5\frac{5}{8}$, $\frac{5}{9}$

Page 53

$\dfrac{4}{7}$, $2\dfrac{1}{2}$, $\dfrac{7}{2}$, $6\dfrac{1}{4}$

$9\dfrac{1}{4}$, $\dfrac{5}{3}$, $6\dfrac{3}{8}$, $\dfrac{3}{2}$

$\dfrac{9}{4}$, $1\dfrac{4}{5}$, $\dfrac{7}{5}$, $8\dfrac{1}{5}$

$2\dfrac{2}{3}$, $\dfrac{13}{7}$, $7\dfrac{1}{7}$, $\dfrac{7}{9}$

$\dfrac{1}{4}$, $3\dfrac{3}{5}$, $\dfrac{7}{4}$, $7\dfrac{4}{7}$

Page 55

$\dfrac{5}{2}$, $9\dfrac{4}{9}$, $\dfrac{1}{7}$, $5\dfrac{1}{2}$

$8\dfrac{1}{3}$, $\dfrac{7}{3}$, $9\dfrac{5}{8}$, $\dfrac{8}{5}$

$\dfrac{6}{5}$, $7\dfrac{1}{2}$, $\dfrac{5}{3}$, $4\dfrac{7}{9}$

$6\dfrac{1}{6}$, $\dfrac{5}{4}$, $8\dfrac{2}{3}$, $\dfrac{5}{6}$

$\dfrac{7}{8}$, $4\dfrac{3}{7}$, $\dfrac{9}{7}$, $9\dfrac{1}{7}$

Page 54

$1\dfrac{3}{8}$, $\dfrac{1}{5}$, $6\dfrac{3}{7}$, $\dfrac{9}{8}$

$\dfrac{4}{7}$, $4\dfrac{5}{6}$, $\dfrac{5}{8}$, $4\dfrac{2}{3}$

$4\dfrac{1}{2}$, $\dfrac{9}{4}$, $6\dfrac{7}{9}$, $\dfrac{5}{2}$

$\dfrac{5}{2}$, $5\dfrac{2}{5}$, $\dfrac{13}{7}$, $4\dfrac{8}{9}$

$9\dfrac{4}{7}$, $\dfrac{9}{8}$, $9\dfrac{1}{6}$, $\dfrac{12}{7}$

Page 56

$8\dfrac{4}{9}$, $\dfrac{5}{4}$, $7\dfrac{7}{8}$, $\dfrac{8}{5}$

$\dfrac{4}{5}$, $7\dfrac{1}{6}$, $\dfrac{1}{5}$, $3\dfrac{3}{7}$

$8\dfrac{2}{3}$, $\dfrac{7}{8}$, $3\dfrac{4}{7}$, $\dfrac{8}{5}$

$\dfrac{3}{8}$, $5\dfrac{4}{7}$, $\dfrac{7}{4}$, $7\dfrac{1}{7}$

$4\dfrac{3}{7}$, $\dfrac{13}{7}$, $7\dfrac{1}{5}$, $\dfrac{7}{6}$

Page 57

$\frac{1}{3}$, $1\frac{1}{4}$, $\frac{1}{9}$, $3\frac{1}{7}$

$6\frac{3}{8}$, $\frac{2}{7}$, $9\frac{2}{3}$, $\frac{7}{6}$

$\frac{5}{2}$, $1\frac{1}{4}$, $\frac{7}{6}$, $8\frac{7}{8}$

$2\frac{1}{3}$, $\frac{1}{4}$, $6\frac{1}{7}$, $\frac{1}{3}$

$\frac{12}{7}$, $9\frac{1}{7}$, $\frac{3}{5}$, $6\frac{6}{7}$

Page 58

$3\frac{8}{9}$, $\frac{8}{3}$, $2\frac{1}{2}$, $\frac{8}{7}$

$\frac{1}{3}$, $3\frac{1}{4}$, $\frac{7}{3}$, $4\frac{1}{2}$

$9\frac{5}{8}$, $\frac{9}{8}$, $7\frac{1}{5}$, $\frac{5}{2}$

$\frac{1}{5}$, $1\frac{3}{4}$, $\frac{1}{4}$, $6\frac{3}{7}$

$1\frac{4}{5}$, $\frac{5}{9}$, $8\frac{1}{6}$, $\frac{5}{9}$

Page 59

$\frac{9}{4}$, $2\frac{5}{9}$, $\frac{3}{2}$, $4\frac{1}{2}$

$5\frac{5}{6}$, $\frac{8}{9}$, $6\frac{1}{3}$, $\frac{2}{3}$

$\frac{5}{7}$, $8\frac{1}{4}$, $\frac{9}{5}$, $2\frac{1}{2}$

$3\frac{1}{7}$, $\frac{7}{4}$, $2\frac{1}{6}$, $\frac{3}{4}$

$\frac{4}{5}$, $1\frac{1}{6}$, $\frac{2}{3}$, $5\frac{5}{7}$

Chapter 6

Page 61

10 , 8 , 18
12 , 8 , 15
12 , 42 , 6
28 , 24 , 72
30 , 40 , 45

Page 62

36 , 6 , 56
20 , 14 , 24
35 , 48 , 18
60 , 21 , 60
18 , 30 , 4

Page 63

60 , 75 , 45
20 , 5 , 60
33 , 60 , 42
36 , 10 , 30
42 , 24 , 24

Page 64

18 , 48 , 56
120 , 14 , 100
20 , 30 , 14
42 , 90 , 30
20 , 40 , 24

Page 65

30 , 12 , 6
21 , 60 , 24
66 , 36 , 90
84 , 54 , 56
18 , 108 , 24

Page 66

60 , 36 , 7
60 , 40 , 24
70 , 72 , 9
72 , 60 , 70
14 , 96 , 20

Page 67

18 , 72 , 48
20 , 84 , 120
96 , 30 , 68
120 , 105 , 15
63 , 200 , 120

Page 68

80 , 60 , 4
42 , 180 , 120
120 , 120 , 40
33 , 6 , 120
36 , 28 , 90

Page 69

84 , 40 , 88
180 , 30 , 60
24 , 84 , 35
20 , 240 , 90
132 , 70 , 40

Page 70

96 , 18 , 56
100 , 18 , 28
12 , 90 , 150
12 , 120 , 24
72 , 48 , 39

Page 71

24 , 84 , 120
108 , 15 , 180
30 , 120 , 42
112 , 24 , 36
12 , 300 , 300

Chapter 7

Page 73

> , < , >
> , > , <
< , > , <
> , > , <
< , > , >

Page 74

> , > , <
> , > , >
< , = , >
> , < , >
> , < , <

Page 75

> , > , >
> , < , <
< , < , <
> , > , >
< , > , <

Page 76

< , < , >
< , < , <
> , > , >
< , < , <
> , < , <

Page 77

> , < , >
> , < , <
< , < , <
> , < , <
< , < , <

Page 78

> , < , >
< , < , <
< , > , <
< , > , =
> , > , =

Page 79

> , > , >
> , > , <
< , < , >
> , < , <
< , < , >

Page 80

> , > , <
= , < , >
> , > , >
> , > , <
< , < , >

Page 81

> , < , >
> , < , <
> , < , >
> , > , <
< , > , >

Page 82

> , > , >
< , > , <
> , < , >
> , > , <
> , > , >

Page 83

< , < , <
< , < , >
> , < , <
> , > , <
< , < , <

Chapter 8

Page 85

$1 \frac{1}{2}$, $14 \frac{11}{15}$, $4 \frac{8}{9}$

$11 \frac{3}{10}$, $3 \frac{5}{6}$, $13 \frac{2}{45}$

$2 \frac{5}{18}$, $9 \frac{31}{40}$, $5 \frac{1}{7}$

Page 86

$3 \frac{1}{12}$, $7 \frac{17}{24}$, $5 \frac{1}{4}$

$8 \frac{17}{30}$, $2 \frac{5}{8}$, $15 \frac{1}{9}$

$2 \frac{1}{14}$, $16 \frac{4}{9}$, $5 \frac{5}{6}$

Page 87

$2 \frac{2}{3}$, $8 \frac{2}{3}$, $6 \frac{3}{4}$

$13 \frac{11}{72}$, $\frac{33}{40}$, $9 \frac{53}{56}$

$3 \frac{1}{12}$, $12 \frac{11}{18}$, $7 \frac{1}{2}$

Page 88

$2 \frac{9}{10}$, $10 \frac{5}{6}$, $8 \frac{3}{7}$

$9 \frac{1}{10}$, $2 \frac{23}{30}$, $8 \frac{5}{42}$

$\frac{59}{63}$, $15 \frac{1}{20}$, $5 \frac{1}{2}$

Page 89

$2 \frac{27}{35}$, $8 \frac{6}{7}$, $8 \frac{7}{9}$

$15 \frac{2}{45}$, $3 \frac{1}{4}$, $9 \frac{13}{18}$

$\frac{23}{45}$, $6 \frac{17}{21}$, $10 \frac{5}{6}$

Page 90

$2 \frac{7}{40}$, $11 \frac{5}{18}$, $3 \frac{4}{5}$

7 , $2 \frac{1}{8}$, 11

$3 \frac{5}{21}$, $2 \frac{9}{20}$, $6 \frac{1}{8}$

Page 91

$2 \frac{13}{15}$, $13 \frac{10}{21}$, $9 \frac{1}{6}$

$10 \frac{1}{12}$, $2 \frac{1}{12}$, $15 \frac{3}{56}$

$1 \frac{1}{6}$, $11 \frac{1}{28}$, $4 \frac{1}{2}$

Page 92

$2 \frac{11}{14}$, $10 \frac{51}{56}$, $8 \frac{1}{6}$

$13 \frac{9}{14}$, $\frac{22}{35}$, $8 \frac{1}{8}$

$2 \frac{2}{3}$, $11 \frac{1}{3}$, $5 \frac{6}{7}$

Page 93

$3 \frac{2}{9}$, $14 \frac{27}{28}$, $3 \frac{3}{8}$

12 , $1 \frac{19}{42}$, $3 \frac{13}{14}$

$4 \frac{9}{10}$, 16 , $12 \frac{1}{2}$

Page 94

$1 \frac{19}{36}$, $9 \frac{1}{18}$, $6 \frac{2}{3}$

$14 \frac{3}{14}$, $1 \frac{23}{45}$, $17 \frac{9}{28}$

$5 \frac{9}{10}$, $7 \frac{3}{10}$, $5 \frac{3}{5}$

Page 95

$1 \frac{7}{24}$, $12 \frac{15}{28}$, $8 \frac{1}{6}$

$14 \frac{2}{5}$, 2 , $8 \frac{3}{28}$

$2 \frac{1}{8}$, $13 \frac{7}{9}$, $10 \frac{1}{4}$

Chapter 9

Page 97

$\dfrac{1}{4}$, $1\dfrac{17}{18}$, $\dfrac{1}{6}$

$1\dfrac{41}{72}$, $2\dfrac{1}{12}$, $2\dfrac{39}{40}$

$\dfrac{31}{63}$, $4\dfrac{1}{9}$, $8\dfrac{8}{9}$

Page 98

$\dfrac{8}{21}$, $5\dfrac{23}{35}$, $\dfrac{1}{7}$

$1\dfrac{34}{63}$, 1 , $\dfrac{1}{12}$

$2\dfrac{1}{36}$, $4\dfrac{17}{42}$, $4\dfrac{6}{7}$

Page 99

$1\dfrac{16}{45}$, $6\dfrac{11}{18}$, $\dfrac{5}{6}$

$4\dfrac{3}{10}$, $\dfrac{19}{24}$, $3\dfrac{2}{3}$

$\dfrac{13}{24}$, $4\dfrac{2}{3}$, $3\dfrac{1}{9}$

Page 100

$1\dfrac{19}{40}$, $3\dfrac{5}{12}$, $\dfrac{5}{6}$

$2\dfrac{3}{4}$, $1\dfrac{5}{14}$, $5\dfrac{17}{28}$

$\dfrac{37}{40}$, $1\dfrac{5}{36}$, $4\dfrac{4}{5}$

Page 101

$\dfrac{17}{36}$, $2\dfrac{3}{4}$, $\dfrac{2}{3}$

$4\dfrac{1}{14}$, $1\dfrac{5}{8}$, $2\dfrac{8}{15}$

$\dfrac{2}{9}$, $\dfrac{13}{14}$, $3\dfrac{2}{3}$

Page 102

$\dfrac{1}{6}$, $1\dfrac{1}{45}$, $\dfrac{1}{8}$

$5\dfrac{7}{8}$, $\dfrac{7}{15}$, $8\dfrac{13}{18}$

$\dfrac{1}{12}$, 4 , $6\dfrac{1}{7}$

Page 103

$\frac{1}{9}$, $4\frac{3}{10}$, $\frac{1}{9}$

$3\frac{5}{14}$, $\frac{2}{3}$, $3\frac{19}{21}$

$\frac{7}{45}$, $7\frac{29}{42}$, $8\frac{3}{4}$

Page 104

$\frac{3}{40}$, $\frac{13}{18}$, $2\frac{1}{2}$

$7\frac{9}{14}$, $\frac{17}{42}$, $\frac{1}{10}$

$\frac{1}{2}$, $3\frac{53}{72}$, $5\frac{1}{7}$

Page 105

$\frac{5}{6}$, $1\frac{1}{8}$, $\frac{1}{9}$

$1\frac{1}{2}$, $1\frac{5}{18}$, $\frac{1}{12}$

$2\frac{13}{18}$, $7\frac{7}{24}$, $\frac{1}{3}$

Page 106

$1\frac{27}{40}$, $\frac{23}{42}$, $\frac{1}{9}$

$3\frac{1}{4}$, $\frac{8}{63}$, $1\frac{5}{9}$

$\frac{8}{35}$, $2\frac{17}{21}$, $\frac{3}{4}$

Page 107

$\frac{1}{2}$, 1 , $\frac{1}{6}$

$3\frac{11}{35}$, $\frac{1}{6}$, 4

$1\frac{9}{10}$, $1\frac{17}{18}$, $7\frac{3}{7}$

Chapter 10

Page 109

$\frac{5}{16}$, $11\frac{31}{49}$, 8

$66\frac{7}{24}$, $1\frac{19}{21}$, $32\frac{11}{54}$

$\frac{45}{56}$, $74\frac{9}{14}$, $\frac{2}{7}$

Page 110

$3\frac{5}{24}$, $13\frac{13}{54}$, 3

$47\frac{5}{6}$, $\frac{5}{6}$, $51\frac{11}{24}$

$\frac{1}{4}$, $14\frac{1}{21}$, $5\frac{1}{3}$

Page 111

$\frac{1}{9}$, $16\frac{1}{2}$, $3\frac{5}{9}$

$29\frac{7}{12}$, $\frac{13}{56}$, $18\frac{17}{18}$

$3\frac{4}{15}$, $47\frac{1}{2}$, $5\frac{1}{3}$

Page 112

$\frac{1}{5}$, $47\frac{1}{5}$, $2\frac{1}{2}$

$14\frac{17}{32}$, $\frac{9}{10}$, $74\frac{2}{5}$

$\frac{27}{40}$, $32\frac{1}{9}$, $1\frac{7}{9}$

Page 113

$\frac{16}{27}$, $27\frac{13}{81}$, $\frac{5}{9}$

$47\frac{45}{64}$, $\frac{3}{10}$, $22\frac{3}{56}$

$\frac{1}{6}$, $34\frac{13}{20}$, $31\frac{1}{2}$

Page 114

$\frac{3}{14}$, $17\frac{3}{5}$, 21

$31\frac{1}{20}$, $2\frac{4}{5}$, $48\frac{5}{12}$

$\frac{7}{16}$, $13\frac{29}{54}$, $2\frac{2}{9}$

Page 115

$3 \frac{1}{5}$, $55 \frac{1}{4}$, $3 \frac{1}{5}$

$40 \frac{5}{18}$, $\frac{1}{2}$, $7 \frac{12}{25}$

$1 \frac{19}{36}$, $70 \frac{8}{9}$, 9

Page 116

$\frac{35}{36}$, 20 , $\frac{2}{5}$

$42 \frac{21}{32}$, $\frac{27}{40}$, $10 \frac{25}{28}$

$5 \frac{1}{4}$, $31 \frac{41}{64}$, $11 \frac{4}{7}$

Page 117

$\frac{49}{54}$, $77 \frac{11}{12}$, $2 \frac{1}{3}$

$35 \frac{1}{21}$, $1 \frac{9}{56}$, $5 \frac{17}{20}$

$\frac{49}{81}$, $51 \frac{29}{81}$, $1 \frac{1}{2}$

Page 118

$\frac{9}{16}$, $31 \frac{5}{12}$, $7 \frac{1}{2}$

$27 \frac{23}{24}$, $1 \frac{2}{7}$, $11 \frac{41}{45}$

$4 \frac{1}{12}$, $19 \frac{3}{7}$, $\frac{2}{3}$

Page 119

$\frac{3}{5}$, $17 \frac{29}{30}$, $12 \frac{5}{6}$

$15 \frac{17}{24}$, $\frac{2}{63}$, $63 \frac{7}{24}$

$1 \frac{11}{24}$, $61 \frac{11}{35}$, $10 \frac{1}{2}$

Chapter 11

Page 121

$$\frac{4}{7} \; , \; \frac{7}{11} \; , \; \frac{4}{5}$$

$$\frac{7}{22} \; , \; \frac{6}{7} \; , \; \frac{6}{11}$$

$$\frac{3}{2} \; , \; \frac{1}{8} \; , \; \frac{4}{9}$$

$$\frac{9}{64} \; , \; \frac{3}{5} \; , \; \frac{6}{49}$$

$$\frac{9}{7} \; , \; \frac{3}{4} \; , \; \frac{7}{8}$$

Page 122

$$\frac{4}{3} \; , \; \frac{9}{23} \; , \; \frac{3}{7}$$

$$\frac{2}{11} \; , \; \frac{2}{3} \; , \; \frac{9}{22}$$

$$6 \; , \; \frac{1}{4} \; , \; 8$$

$$\frac{4}{29} \; , \; \frac{5}{7} \; , \; \frac{3}{16}$$

$$\frac{4}{3} \; , \; \frac{9}{43} \; , \; 3$$

Page 123

$$\frac{6}{11} \; , \; \frac{5}{33} \; , \; \frac{6}{5}$$

$$\frac{8}{47} \; , \; \frac{6}{7} \; , \; \frac{2}{9}$$

$$\frac{2}{9} \; , \; \frac{1}{7} \; , \; \frac{5}{7}$$

$$\frac{6}{31} \; , \; \frac{5}{6} \; , \; \frac{6}{49}$$

$$\frac{9}{2} \; , \; \frac{4}{33} \; , \; 8$$

Page 124

$$\frac{2}{9} \; , \; \frac{5}{48} \; , \; 4$$

$$\frac{8}{39} \; , \; \frac{4}{7} \; , \; \frac{8}{49}$$

$$\frac{3}{2} \; , \; \frac{1}{2} \; , \; 9$$

$$\frac{4}{27} \; , \; \frac{8}{3} \; , \; \frac{2}{13}$$

$$\frac{2}{7} \; , \; \frac{7}{61} \; , \; \frac{3}{7}$$

Page 125

$$4 \; , \; \frac{5}{44} \; , \; \frac{3}{4}$$

$$\frac{9}{59} \; , \; \frac{7}{6} \; , \; \frac{7}{37}$$

$$6 \; , \; \frac{1}{6} \; , \; \frac{5}{2}$$

$$\frac{4}{7} \; , \; \frac{6}{11} \; , \; \frac{8}{39}$$

$$\frac{5}{3} \; , \; \frac{9}{28} \; , \; \frac{9}{2}$$

Page 126

$$3 \; , \; \frac{7}{17} \; , \; \frac{3}{4}$$

$$\frac{8}{49} \; , \; 2 \; , \; \frac{6}{13}$$

$$\frac{2}{9} \; , \; \frac{1}{7} \; , \; \frac{2}{7}$$

$$\frac{2}{7} \; , \; \frac{6}{7} \; , \; \frac{8}{43}$$

$$\frac{3}{5} \; , \; \frac{8}{39} \; , \; \frac{5}{3}$$

Page 127

8 , $\dfrac{8}{21}$, $\dfrac{2}{3}$

$\dfrac{9}{71}$, $\dfrac{2}{3}$, $\dfrac{8}{73}$

$\dfrac{9}{4}$, $\dfrac{1}{9}$, $\dfrac{5}{2}$

$\dfrac{6}{37}$, $\dfrac{3}{7}$, $\dfrac{5}{7}$

$\dfrac{5}{4}$, $\dfrac{2}{9}$, 4

Page 128

9 , $\dfrac{5}{16}$, $\dfrac{8}{9}$

$\dfrac{6}{31}$, $\dfrac{7}{13}$, $\dfrac{7}{57}$

$\dfrac{4}{9}$, $\dfrac{1}{4}$, $\dfrac{7}{11}$

$\dfrac{8}{11}$, $\dfrac{3}{7}$, $\dfrac{2}{7}$

$\dfrac{8}{7}$, $\dfrac{7}{60}$, $\dfrac{5}{8}$

Page 129

$\dfrac{7}{8}$, $\dfrac{5}{49}$, $\dfrac{9}{8}$

$\dfrac{9}{40}$, $\dfrac{6}{7}$, $\dfrac{7}{59}$

$\dfrac{2}{7}$, $\dfrac{1}{8}$, $\dfrac{3}{8}$

$\dfrac{7}{32}$, 8 , $\dfrac{3}{20}$

8 , $\dfrac{3}{5}$, 4

Page 130

$\dfrac{4}{3}$, $\dfrac{7}{30}$, $\dfrac{5}{3}$

$\dfrac{6}{43}$, 8 , $\dfrac{8}{11}$

$\dfrac{6}{5}$, $\dfrac{1}{9}$, $\dfrac{7}{9}$

$\dfrac{4}{35}$, $\dfrac{2}{7}$, $\dfrac{9}{37}$

$\dfrac{7}{10}$, $\dfrac{9}{83}$, $\dfrac{7}{12}$

Page 131

$\dfrac{7}{13}$, $\dfrac{2}{9}$, $\dfrac{7}{3}$

$\dfrac{4}{5}$, $\dfrac{5}{8}$, $\dfrac{5}{8}$

$\dfrac{3}{5}$, $\dfrac{1}{2}$, $\dfrac{3}{8}$

$\dfrac{5}{6}$, $\dfrac{6}{7}$, $\dfrac{3}{8}$

5 , $\dfrac{2}{3}$, $\dfrac{7}{8}$

Chapter 12

Page 133

1 , $2\frac{1}{46}$, $\frac{5}{24}$

$\frac{43}{69}$, $\frac{9}{56}$, $1\frac{53}{136}$

6 , $1\frac{4}{19}$, $22\frac{1}{2}$

Page 134

$\frac{8}{15}$, $1\frac{11}{54}$, $\frac{11}{18}$

$1\frac{49}{117}$, 4 , $\frac{80}{287}$

$1\frac{1}{3}$, $\frac{54}{155}$, 9

Page 135

$2\frac{1}{2}$, $\frac{11}{14}$, $\frac{4}{21}$

$1\frac{1}{8}$, $2\frac{1}{12}$, $\frac{396}{427}$

$\frac{5}{18}$, $3\frac{1}{28}$, $13\frac{1}{2}$

Page 136

$\frac{60}{77}$, $1\frac{19}{30}$, $\frac{5}{18}$

$2\frac{19}{34}$, $7\frac{3}{7}$, $1\frac{157}{329}$

$1\frac{13}{42}$, $\frac{20}{59}$, $4\frac{4}{5}$

Page 137

$15\frac{3}{7}$, $\frac{13}{17}$, $\frac{3}{4}$

$1\frac{29}{70}$, $1\frac{7}{8}$, $1\frac{11}{40}$

11 , $\frac{55}{172}$, 42

Page 138

$20\frac{1}{4}$, $5\frac{23}{27}$, $\frac{3}{4}$

$1\frac{5}{27}$, $\frac{24}{55}$, $2\frac{71}{117}$

$1\frac{5}{16}$, $1\frac{19}{116}$, $\frac{2}{7}$

Page 139

$\frac{28}{81}$, $\frac{155}{306}$, $\frac{1}{48}$

$\frac{58}{117}$, $\frac{14}{25}$, $2\frac{7}{19}$

2, $2\frac{59}{261}$, $3\frac{3}{7}$

Page 140

16, $\frac{32}{51}$, $\frac{3}{14}$

$2\frac{50}{87}$, $\frac{4}{5}$, $\frac{31}{34}$

$1\frac{5}{9}$, $\frac{17}{25}$, $3\frac{1}{2}$

Page 141

$1\frac{1}{6}$, $\frac{77}{354}$, $\frac{5}{18}$

$\frac{203}{205}$, $1\frac{1}{9}$, $6\frac{8}{11}$

$2\frac{25}{28}$, $\frac{117}{268}$, 18

Page 142

$\frac{2}{7}$, $\frac{10}{21}$, $\frac{5}{14}$

$\frac{80}{99}$, $2\frac{2}{15}$, $1\frac{11}{15}$

1, $4\frac{31}{36}$, 48

Page 143

$2\frac{14}{15}$, $\frac{91}{100}$, $\frac{12}{35}$

$1\frac{325}{387}$, $\frac{5}{8}$, $1\frac{25}{33}$

$1\frac{4}{7}$, $4\frac{2}{7}$, 56

Made in the USA
Las Vegas, NV
01 September 2021